Heinemann EXPLORE Science

Teacher's Book

New International Edition

Grade 3

Tara Lievesley, Deborah Herridge
Series editor: John Stringer

AYS LEARNING

PEARSON

Pearson Education Limited is a company incorporated in England and Wales having its registered office at Edinburgh Gate, Harlow, Essex, CM20 2JE.

Registered company number: 872828

Text © Pearson Education Limited 2012
First published 2003. This edition published 2012.

www.pearsonglobalschools.com

16 15 14 13 12
IMP 10 9 8 7 6 5 4 3 2 1

British Library Cataloguing in Publication Data
A catalogue record for this book is available from the British Library

ISBN 978 0 43513 364 1

Edited by Pat Winfield
Designed by Techset Ltd, Gateshead
Original illustrations © Pearson Education Limited, 2003, 2009, 2012
Illustrated by TechSet Ltd, Gateshead
Cover photo/illustration © Alamy Images
Printed in China (SWTC/01)

Acknowledgements
Every effort has been made to contact copyright holders of material reproduced in this book. Any omissions will be rectified in subsequent printings if notice is given to the publishers.

Contents

New International Edition

Introduction

Heinemann Explore Science New International Edition provides a comprehensive, easy-to-use resource written especially for the international primary classroom.

The teaching framework follows the Cambridge International Examinations Primary Science Curriculum Framework (2011), enabling you to minimize planning. The simple structure of *Heinemann Explore Science* gives you flexibility to teach the Units within a Grade in the order that suits your situation.

There is one Unit for each half of a term, with multiple lessons in that Unit. The first lesson in each Unit is an introduction and the last one is a plenary. The other lessons either focus on knowledge and understanding or on manageable, tried and tested investigation activities.
The greater the opportunity for investigation, the more practical lessons there are.

Each Grade of *Heinemann Explore Science* contains in the *Teacher's Book* detailed teacher's notes, which provide all the resources you need for planning and delivering successful science lessons. It also includes an accompanying *Student Book* to bring the science topics to life for the children; a *Workbook* with activities to do at school or at home, and six *Readers* to develop students' English language skills through science. Alongside these components, digital resources available via online subscription at www.heinemannexplore. co.uk provide an e-book version of the printed books, opportunities for independent research into the Biology, Chemistry and Physics covered in the scheme and further activities and simulations.

This unique combination of science and ICT stimulates students and enables you to deliver enriching science lessons using today's technology.

Heinemann Explore Science and English language development

Science and language development have much in common. In both, students are frequently highly motivated. Science is a popular subject area in primary schools with students (and with teachers!), and produces interesting and engaging results. Language and science are both social activities. Students' language will not develop without co-operation and collaboration, and science is also a collaborative subject. Finally, science experiences can lead, as few other subjects do, to a desire to communicate discoveries.

When developing spoken English, remember:

- Discussion can be stimulated by working in threes. Two friends doing science may have a common and familiar way of communicating. Three extends the discussion.
- Snowball or jigsaw activities, in which groups share and exchange information, are engaging.
- Discussion before and after an investigation can clarify thoughts. Having to explain what students discovered in their investigation helps clarify thinking and improve language skills.
- Presenting results to others imposes a discipline as well as giving purpose to recording and to clear presentation.
- Reading can be developed through following instructions – including safety instructions – and using the *Student Book* and targeted *Readers*.

Students may be understandably reluctant to record their discoveries. When encouraging written recording, use a variety of recording methods.

- Writing to a structure helps to order students' thoughts.
- Annotated diagrams are an effective way of recording practical science – used by adult scientists as well as students.
- A recorded observation alone may lead to a conclusion.
- Ordering and recording whole investigations is difficult, and can often be better done to a writing framework.

Heinemann Explore Science offers and defines new vocabulary. If the words are new to you, or you have any doubts yourself about their definition, use the definitions in the Glossary in the *Student Book*.

- Draw the students' attention to the new words.
- Depending on the students' age, set them to illustrate or define the words themselves. Introduce word games – matching the word to the definition.
- Make a 'Words of Science' poster or a class dictionary.

- Ask the students to use the words in context; to act them out; to guess which word you are thinking of, either by 20 questions or by giving clues.
- Use cloze procedure to place new words.

Components of the scheme

The **Heinemann Explore Science** *Teacher's Book* provides detailed guidance on teaching with the corresponding sections of the *Student Book* pages. Used alongside the electronic components, where you will find a variety of resources for planning and teaching, the *Teacher's Book* is the main starting point for any lesson. Each Unit provides approximately a half-term's worth of work – an introduction, and almost always four lesson plans (each of which may be taught in a single session or across science sessions during the week), and a final review.

Each Unit introduction provides:

1   Clear background science information to support the non-specialist teacher.

2   Simple definitions of necessary scientific vocabulary.

3   A complete list of resources needed in the Unit.

4   Helpful hints on prior preparation or useful additional resources.

5   Indications of what students should already know and be able to do before starting the Unit.

6   Cross-curricular references to other subject areas.

7   A discussion question to set the scene and introduce a context for the Unit.

There are two types of lesson in **Heinemann Explore Science**. The first type focuses on knowledge and understanding objectives. These lessons contain:

1   Starter activities to initiate whole-class discussion. Questioning will enable you to establish what the students already know.

2   References to the corresponding *Student Book* pages and further information to expand on the paragraphs in the *Student Book*.

3   Safety tips to advise of specific hazards where appropriate.

4   Additional information necessary for the activities in the 'Things to do' section of the *Student Book*, plus suggestions of how to differentiate and record. Any worksheets required are cross-referenced.

5   Integrated ICT research activities using the website.

6   Further details or extra 'fun facts' to support those listed in the *Student Book*.

7   The answer to the 'I wonder…' question, with additional background explanation if necessary.

8   More activities that can be used instead of, or as well as, those in the 'Things to do' section.

9   Ideas for how students could present their work or tips for classroom displays are provided on the website to help students.

10   Suggestions for homework activities.

11   An activity or series of questions to reinforce the main objectives in the plenary session, drawing the lesson to a close.

The second type of lesson offers a challenge to encourage students to use scientific enquiry skills to investigate a problem in context. These contain:

1   Starter activities to initiate whole-class discussion.

2   A challenge introduced in context, explaining what students will be investigating.

3   Safety tips advising of unique hazards where appropriate; an individual risk assessment is always recommended.

4   Further details of how to carry out the investigation, supporting the instructions in the *Student Book*.

5   Lists of materials students will need, including any to be prepared in advance.

6   Explanations of what students should be looking for, or how to keep the test fair. How best to support and extend students.

7   How to organize, record, analyze and present data collected in the investigation. Suitable tables for data recording are provided as worksheets in the *Workbook*.

8   Students are encouraged to review how well they carried out their investigation and how good their results were. Using the report provided for each investigation helps students build evaluation skills by criticizing methods and conclusions.

9 A different scenario is offered to enable students to apply what they have learned.

10 Additional activities can be used instead of, or as well as, the investigative challenge.

11 Suggestions for homework activities.

12 An activity or series of questions to reinforce the main objectives in the plenary session draw the lesson to a close.

At the end of each Unit, material is provided for an assessment and review lesson:

1 A clear summary of the knowledge and skills students have gained through the Unit divided into three levels of attainment.

2 Explanation and expected responses to the 'Check-up' in the *Student Book*.

3 Answers to the assessment worksheets in the *Workbook*.

4 The answer to the original question posed at the beginning of the Unit.

5 A final activity completes the Unit and reminds students of everything they have learned.

In addition, there are six readers for each Grade of the Framework. These are written to match the appropriate science for the Grade, but with close attention to language levels. Students can learn English language through science, and science through practising their English.

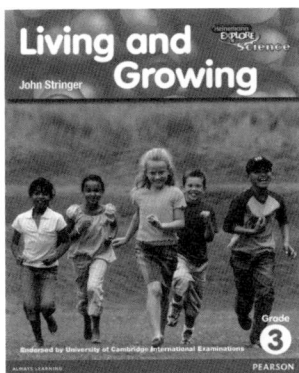

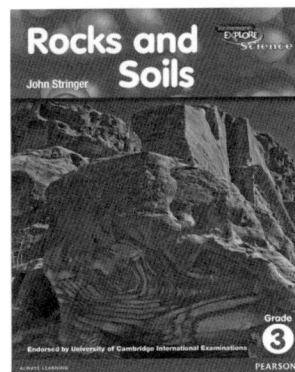

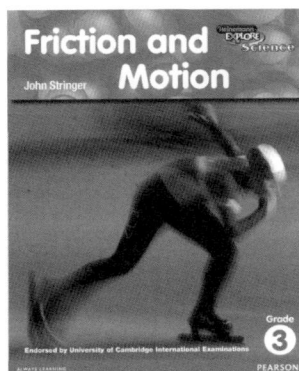

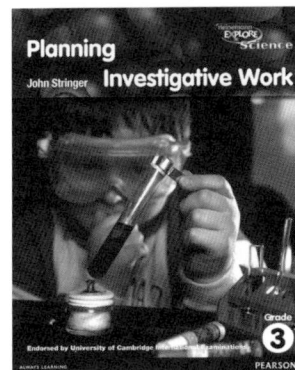

Living and Growing
John Stringer
Grade 3
PEARSON

Helping Plants Grow Well
John Stringer
Grade 3
PEARSON

Properties of Materials
John Stringer
Grade 3
PEARSON

Rocks and Soils
John Stringer
Grade 3
PEARSON

Friction and Motion
John Stringer
Grade 3
PEARSON

Planning Investigative Work
John Stringer
Grade 3
PEARSON

New International Edition

Quick guide to the *Teacher's Book*

The **Heinemann Explore Science** *Grade 3 Teacher's Book* provides detailed guidance on teaching with the corresponding sections of the *Student Book* pages. Used alongside the e-book, the *Teacher's Book* is the main starting point for any lesson. Each Unit provides approximately one half-term's worth of work and comprises an introduction and generally six or seven lessons (each of which may be taught all at once, or across a number of science sessions during the week), plus a review.

Each Unit introduction provides:

3 Useful definitions of scientific vocabulary commonly misunderstood by students.

4 Helpful hints on prior preparation or useful resources.

2 Clear background science information to support the non-specialist teacher.

5 Specific references to other subject areas.

1 A complete list of resources needed throughout the unit.

6 Indicators of what students should know and be able to do before starting this Unit.

7 An initial discussion question to set the scene and introduce a context for the Unit.

There are two types of lesson in *Heinemann Explore Science*. The first type focuses on knowledge and understanding objectives.

2 Safety tips warn of possible hazards where appropriate.

3 Integrated ICT activities using the accompanying e-book or the Internet.

4 The answer to the 'I wonder...' question, with additional background explanations if necessary.

1 Starter activities initiate whole-class discussion. Questioning will enable you to find out what the students already know.

5 Ideas for how students could present their work or tips for classroom displays.

11 References to the corresponding *Student Book* pages and further information to expand on the paragraphs in the *Student Book*.

6 Suggestions for homework activities.

10 Any additional information necessary for the activities in the 'Things to do' section of the *Student Book*, plus suggestions of how to differentiate and record.

9 Further details or extra 'fun facts' to support those listed in the *Student Book*.

8 More activities that can be used instead of or as well as those in the 'Things to do' section.

7 An activity or series of questions to help reinforce the main objectives in the plenary session to draw the lesson to a close.

The second type of lesson offers a challenge to encourage students to use their scientific enquiry skills to investigate a problem in context.

1 Starter activities initiate whole-class discussion.

2 The challenge introduces the context and explains what students will be investigating.

3 Safety tips warn of possible hazards where appropriate.

4 Further details of how to carry out the investigation to support the instructions to the students in the *Student Book*.

5 List of materials that students will need, including any that need to be prepared in advance.

6 Explanations of what students should be looking for and noticing, or how they should keep the tests fair. Ideas on how to support and extend students are also included.

7 Information on how to organize, record, analyse and present data collected in the investigation. Tables for recording results and exemplar data to convert into charts or graphs can be found in the *Student Book* and *Workbook*.

8 Students are encouraged to review how well they carried out their investigation and how good their results were. Use the report provided for each investigation to help students build evaluation skills by criticizing methods and conclusions.

9 Present students with a different scenario to enable them to apply what they have learned.

10 More activities that can be used instead of or as well as the investigative challenge.

11 Suggestions for homework activities.

12 An activity or series of questions to help reinforce the main objectives in the plenary session to draw the lesson to a close.

At the end of each unit, material is provided for an assessment and review lesson.

1 A clear summary of the knowledge and skills students have gained throughout the unit.

2 Explanation and expected responses to the Check-up in the *Student Book*.

3 Assessment sheets can be found in the *Workbook* and e-book.

4 The answer to the original question posed at the beginning of the unit. Discuss what the students think now in light of what they have learned.

5 A final activity completes the unit to remind students of everything they have learned.

6 Answers to *Workbook* end of unit assessments.

How to use
Heinemann Explore Science

For ease of use, **Heinemann Explore Science** follows the structure of the Cambridge Primary Science Curriculum Framework, 2011. **Heinemann Explore Science** has been written so that you can be flexible about what you teach and when.

Heinemann Explore Science is more manageable than many primary science schemes. It has a simple structure, but it also offers wide investigative and research opportunities. A range of engaging tasks is offered for each topic, including practical and research-based activities. Its clear progression and layout offers more support to less confident teachers. Integrated assessment gives indications of how to interpret levels of attainment. There is support for differentiation with suggestions for extra challenges for bright students and support for students struggling with science concepts. There is both experimental and investigative science through reliable practical investigations.

Heinemann Explore Science emphasizes: investigations; the clear use of strong vocabulary lists; building on students' ideas and addressing common misconceptions through questioning and discussion; clearly identified support and extend activities; class demonstration as a basis for some practical activities; and appropriate activities as part of students' homework. It offers flexibility of use; although Units are ordered to match the CIE, they can be taught in any order to suit a school's own scheme of work. This helps in mixed-age classes.

Differentiation

Within any class there will be a wide range of experience and ability. In a mixed-age class that range is further extended. This is a challenge to any teacher, and many address it through careful differentiation. Commonly, work is planned for a number of different groups (often three: high achievers, a middle range group, and students needing additional support). Teachers then allocate their resources – human and practical – to these groups to ensure the best possible outcome for everybody. This 'planning for differentiation' is demanding, and may leave feelings of dissatisfaction – 'I didn't spend long enough with the high-fliers/slower group today', 'I hope I'm not neglecting the majority of the class'. Some teachers have similar difficulties with 'differentiation by outcome'. Less able students may be unchallenged by the assumption that they will always produce a few lines of text when others routinely write a page.

Heinemann Explore Science expects that you will need to differentiate your work, and so a range of resources is offered, any of which may stimulate particular groups. You may choose to: present an activity on an investigation table, possibly supported by an informed adult; to set out resources that students can use for creative play; or to use the *Student Book* or *Workbook* for stimulus, for direction or for recording.

The 'starting off' activities in **Heinemann Explore Science** invite a third form of differentiation: differentiation by presentation. This is so familiar to teachers that few recognize how effectively they use it. The way in which a topic is presented engages students, but it also enables you to assess their prior knowledge. Because of its practical nature, students who may not shine in other subjects will often contribute more in science. Students who are able in every respect may still surprise you with their knowledge, but this 'knowledge' needs to be probed carefully – a superficial knowledge may lack the depth of understanding on which new science learning can be built.

That's why **Heinemann Explore Science** includes a number of exemplar questions to elicit current understanding – whether it is insecure, or even whether students have misconceptions that need gently challenging. It is when you group the students and set the tasks that you 'differentiate by presentation' – an unconscious and instinctive skill that results in different groups busily engaged with differing levels of support and monitoring.

Level statements to help you identify at which level students are working are provided in this *Teacher's Book*, for each Unit. These are also provided at the back of the *Student Book* for discussion and as checklists to enable self-assessment by students.

Heinemann Explore Science contains a wide range of ideas for interaction that includes things to do, questions to ask and resources to support learning. Your professional role is in the effective deployment of those resources.

The Heinemann Explore Science website

This provides a full range of editable planning materials, generic writing frames and presentation templates to support students in recording and presenting their work.

The website also provides digital e-book versions of all the *Readers* for each Grade and for the *Student Books* and *Workbooks*, so that worksheets can be downloaded and printed if needed.

Using ICT for research

Students should develop their research skills using a variety of secondary sources. Throughout the *Student Book*, students are given opportunities to use ICT to research the answers to questions related to the topic of the lesson. At the end of each Unit, a more open question with reference only to the appropriate area of study is introduced to encourage students to develop search skills and strategies.

The Heinemann Explore Science Readers

These have been written bearing in mind the language needs of students for whom English is not a first language. Each book complements a Unit in the scheme. They offer interesting illustrations and simple, engaging text. Word count increases with higher Grades. They can be used as individual readers, books to read at home, or for group reading. They can be used for vocabulary and language exercise, and there are suggestions for activities at the back of each book – from crosswords to team games.

Used alongside the other components of the scheme, they offer opportunities for developing science and language, hand in hand.

Health and safety issues

Primary science is a very safe activity, but that does not mean that you should not consider health and safety issues when you plan, or that you should feel unsupported, either. *Heinemann Explore Science* highlights specific safety issues in lessons when appropriate, and you should also engage in your own risk assessment and take appropriate precautions. This should not be demanding; it involves looking at your students, your circumstances and support staff, and ensuring that you have noted, minimized and if necessary recorded any apparent hazards. It is essential to share this risk assessment with other adults in the classroom.

Every adult on the school site should be familiar with the school's Health and Safety Policy, and especially how it reflects on their responsibilities. They should know the location and proper use of safety equipment. All adults have a responsibility for their own safety, and that of their students in school, whatever their age. This is a responsibility you share with others. Teaching assistants, for example, are often responsible for small groups of students doing practical activities – their supervision may be vital where a hazard has been recognized, for example, when using a cooker. Working with a small group like this offers opportunities not just for realistic but negative teaching ('Don't touch that – it's hot!') but also for positive modelling of safe behaviour ('Now how should I pick this up?').

You can give a very positive image of health and safety issues by performing a routine risk assessment while planning an activity, and encouraging students to make their own assessment of risk, and take their own precautions. Engaging students in safety planning helps them to understand the importance of not taking risks. If students are simply told what is safe without explanation they are less likely to take it as seriously as when they are themselves involved in safety planning.

Here are a few general common-sense reminders:

Food: Eating and drinking is forbidden in school science labs, but some of primary science is concerned with food – science activities may require students to eat, but only with your permission. Fingers do get sucked, and foods are tempting. Ensure that guidelines on 'what to eat' are clear and take into account ethnicity, custom, parental wishes and allergies.

New International Edition

Present the best practice in food handling: the cleaning and/or covering of tables, and the use of cooking utensils kept only for this purpose. Pupils should know not to enter the food area unless they are in the practical group (mark or point out an area that can only be entered with clean hands and wearing an apron). Protective clothing not only keeps the students' clothes clean but also prevents food contamination. It should be kept solely for food use. PVC aprons or smocks (coveralls) can be cleaned by wiping with an antibacterial cleaner. Washable aprons should be hot washed at least once a term.

Laminated plastic tables are ideal. Wooden tables (or damaged laminated tables) should be covered with clean plastic tablecloths kept specifically for food. Older students can use antibacterial cleaners after an initial thorough clean by an adult. Spray or wipe all food preparation surfaces including chopping boards with the antibacterial cleaner, wipe clean and leave to dry before using.

Nobody – pupil or adult – should work with food if they are unwell, including sickness, diarrhoea, colds, coughs and other infections. Cuts must be covered with a clean waterproof dressing – blue plasters show up if they drop into food! Supervise students washing hands before food work, or after using the toilet. Provide colourless, perfume-free liquid soap and running water. If a hot air dryer is not available, provide disposable paper towels or paper roller towels. Discourage students from touching their face, hair or other parts of their body, and from coughing or sneezing over food.

Electricity: Teach students about the dangers of mains electricity. Students live with electricity and refusing them experience of it is comparable to not teaching them road safety rules for fear of traffic accidents. Mains electricity has a far greater 'push' round the circuit than battery electricity. It is this greater push that kills. The human body is not a good conductor of electricity, but it conducts electricity far better when wet. Work with low-voltage 'battery' electricity is not risky.

Forces: Many activities in science (and technology) put students at risk because little thought is given to possible outcomes. What will happen if the elastic band snaps, the bag breaks, or the liquid spills? Students may take unnecessary risks too, by not using basic science equipment (eye protection, a cutting board or bench hook)

that could keep them safe. Testing-to-breaking-point activities in topics such as Forces can be dangerous unless students have considered the consequences of breakage.

Animals: The key factor is the welfare of both students and animals. The learning outcome is an understanding of animal welfare and a positive educational experience of (say) a small mammal. It's important to ensure that none of the students has an allergy to animal fur. If you introduce family pets, it's unlikely that they are used to being surrounded by a group of excited students.

Introduce any animal to a group/class yourself. Talk about them, drawing out what the students know, and what they think about how the animal might behave. Students empathize with small animals, and will understand that they could be easily frightened.

The adult should handle the animal throughout the group activity. Students could ask their questions first, and then take it in turns to stroke the animal at the end, which reduces the chances that students will go rubbing their eyes or sucking their fingers afterwards! After their experience, they should wash their hands again, under supervision.

General advice: Younger students can be expected to be able to control risks to themselves and others. They commonly know what is dangerous. Classroom accidents are frequently the result of students forgetting what is sensible because they are caught up in an activity, especially if it is exciting science!

Essential safety advice is contained in a book from the Association for Science Education called *'Be Safe!'* and every teacher should be aware of it and its contents. *Be Safe!* is available from The Association for Science Education, College Lane, Hatfield, Herts. AL10 9AA, UK

www.ase.org.uk
Be Safe! ISBN: 978 0 86357 426 9

CLEAPSS is the advisory service for health and safety in science education. CLEAPSS offers informative publications, a staffed helpline, and a members' website. It is an essential source of science safety knowledge.

www.cleapss.org.uk

Curriculum structure of *Heinemann Explore Science*

Heinemann Explore Science has been very carefully structured to ensure a progressive development in the students using the course, both of scientific process skills and also of knowledge and understanding. This complements the approach taken in the Cambridge Primary Science Curriculum.

The development of scientific process skills throughout the complete course is shown in this skills ladder:

Heinemann Explore Science Science Skills Ladder

Skills Domain	Year 1 Children have opportunities:	Year 2 Children have opportunities:	Year 3 Children have opportunities:	Year 4 Children have opportunities:	Year 5 Children have opportunities:	Year 6 Children have opportunities:
1. **Ideas and evidence in science**	to collect evidence to try to answer a question	to collect evidence to try to answer a question	to collect evidence in a variety of contexts to answer a question or test an idea	to collect evidence in a variety of contexts to test an idea or prediction based on their scientific knowledge and understanding	to consider how scientists have combined evidence from observation and measurement with creative thinking to suggest new ideas and explanations for phenomena	to consider how scientists have combined evidence from observation and measurement with creative thinking to suggest new ideas and explanations for phenomena
2. **Investigative skills** **Planning investigative work**	to test ideas suggested to them and say what they think will happen	to suggest some ideas and questions based on simple knowledge and say how they might find out about them; to say what they think might happen; and to think about and discuss whether comparisons and tests are fair or unfair	in a variety of contexts, to suggest questions and ideas and how to test them; to make predictions about what will happen; to think about how to collect sufficient evidence in some contexts; and to consider what makes a test unfair or evidence sufficient and, with help, plan fair tests	to suggest questions that can be tested and make predictions about what will happen, some of which are based on scientific knowledge; to design a fair test or plan how to collect sufficient evidence; and, in some contexts, to choose what apparatus to use and what to measure	to make predictions of what will happen based on scientific knowledge and understanding, and suggest how to test these; to use knowledge and understanding to plan how to carry out a fair test or how to collect sufficient evidence to test an idea; and to identify factors that need to be taken into consideration in different contexts	to decide how to turn ideas into a form that can be tested and, where appropriate, to make predictions using scientific knowledge and understanding; to identify factors that are relevant to a particular situation; to choose what evidence to collect to investigate a question, ensuring the evidence is sufficient; and to choose what equipment to use

New International Edition

Heinemann Explore Science Science Skills Ladder

Skills Domain	Year 1 Children have opportunities:	Year 2 Children have opportunities:	Year 3 Children have opportunities:	Year 4 Children have opportunities:	Year 5 Children have opportunities:	Year 6 Children have opportunities:
3. **Obtaining and presenting evidence**		to make observations using appropriate senses; to make some measurements of length using standard and non-standard measures; and to present some findings in simple tables and block graphs	to make observations and comparisons; to measure length, volume of liquid and time in standard measures using simple measuring equipment effectively; and to present results in drawing, bar charts and tables	to make observations and comparisons of relevant features in a variety of contexts; to make measurements of temperature, time and force as well as measurements of length; to begin to think about why measurements of length should be repeated; and to present results in bar charts and tables	to make relevant observations; to consolidate measurement of volume, temperature, time and length; to measure pulse rate; to think about why observations and measurements should be repeated; and to present results in bar charts and line graphs	to make a variety of relevant observations and measurements using simple apparatus correctly; to decide when observations and measurements need to be checked, by repeating, to give more reliable data; and to use tables, bar charts and line graphs to present results
4. **Considering evidence and approach**	to communicate observations orally, in drawing, by labelling and in simple writing; to make simple comparisons and groupings that relate to differences and similarities between living things and objects; in some cases to say what their observations show, and whether it was what they expected; and to draw simple conclusions and explain what they did	to make simple comparisons, identifying similarities and differences between living things, objects and events; to say what results show; to say whether their predictions were supported; in some cases to use knowledge to explain what was found out and to draw conclusions; and to explain what they did	to draw conclusions from results and begin to use scientific knowledge to suggest explanations for them; and to make generalizations and begin to identify simple patterns in results presented in tables	to identify simple trends and patterns in results presented in tables, charts and graphs and to suggest explanations for some of these; to explain what the evidence shows and whether it supports any predictions made; and to link the evidence to scientific knowledge and understanding in some contexts	to decide whether results support any prediction; to begin to evaluate repeated results; to recognize and make predictions from patterns in data and suggest explanations for these using scientific knowledge and understanding; to interpret data and think about whether it is sufficient to draw conclusions; and to draw conclusions indicating whether these match any prediction made	to make comparisons; to evaluate repeated results; to identify patterns in results and results that do not appear to fit the pattern; to use results to draw conclusions and to make further predictions; to suggest and evaluate explanations for these predictions using scientific knowledge and understanding; and to say whether the evidence supports any prediction made

Heinemann Explore Science Curriculum Matching Chart for Grade 3

This chart shows where all of the topics and Learning Objectives specified in the Cambridge Primary Science Curriculum are covered in the *Heinemann Explore Science* course.

Learning Objectives	*Student Book* coverage	Supporting coverage in *Teacher's Book* or *Workbook*
Scientific enquiry		
Scientific enquiry: Ideas and evidence		
Collect evidence in a variety of contexts to answer questions or test ideas.	Unit 2: Helping plants grow well • Plants and water, pp.30–1	*Teacher's Book* 3, pp.40–57
	Unit 4: Rocks and soils • Hard rocks pp.58–9 • Types of soil pp.60-1 • Testing soils pp.62–3 • Soil and water pp.64–5	*Teacher's Book* 3, pp.74–89
	Unit 5: Magnets and springs • Strength of magnets pp.72–3 • Stretching and squeezing pp.74–5	*Teacher's Book* 3, pp.90–105
Scientific enquiry: Plan investigative work		
Suggest ideas, make predictions and communicate these.	Unit 1: Living and growing • Clean teeth pp.20–1	*Teacher's Book* 3, pp.16–39
	Unit 2: Helping plants grow well • Growing plants, pp.26–7 • Plants and water, pp.30–1 • Unit 2 Review, p.38	*Teacher's Book* 3, pp.40–57
	Unit 3: Characteristics of materials • Building bridges pp.44–5 • Exploring paper pp.48–9 • Stretchy materials pp.50–1	*Teacher's Book* 3, pp.58–73
	Unit 4: Rocks and soils • Sorting rocks pp.56–7 • Hard rocks pp.58–9 • Testing soils pp.62–3 • Soil and water pp.64–5	*Teacher's Book* 3, pp.74–89
	Unit 5: Magnets and springs • Strength of magnets pp.72–3 • Exploring springs pp.76–7	*Teacher's Book* 3, pp.90–105
	Unit 6: Friction • Unit 6: pp.85, 87, 91, 93	*Teacher's Book* 3, pp.106–121
With help, think about collecting evidence and planning fair tests.	Unit 1: Living and growing • Clean teeth pp.20–1	*Teacher's Book* 3, pp.16–39
	Unit 2: Helping plants grow well • Growing plants pp.26–7 • Plants and water pp.30–1	*Teacher's Book* 3, pp.40–57
	Unit 4: Rocks and soils • Hard rocks pp.58–9 • Testing soils pp.62–3 • Soil and water pp.64–5	*Teacher's Book* 3, pp.74–89
	Unit 5: Magnets and springs • Magnetic materials pp.70–1 • Strength of magnets pp.72–3 • Spring power pp.78–9	*Teacher's Book* 3, pp.90–105
	Unit 6: Friction • Measuring forces pp.84–5 • Slippery surfaces pp.86–7 • Exploring friction pp.92–3	*Teacher's Book* 3, pp.106–121

11

Scientific enquiry: Obtain and present evidence		
Observe and compare objects, living things and events.	Unit 4: Rocks and soils • Types of soil pp.60–1 • Testing soils pp.62–3	*Teacher's Book* 3, pp.74–89
	Unit 6: Friction • Testing spinners pp.90–1	*Teacher's Book* 3, pp.106–121
Measure using simple equipment and record observations in a variety of ways.	Unit 1: Living and growing • Clean teeth pp.20–1	*Teacher's Book* 3, pp.16–39
	Unit 2: Helping plants grow well • Growing plants pp.26–7 • Plants and water pp.30–1	*Teacher's Book* 3, pp.40–57
	Unit 3: Characteristics of materials • Stretchy materials pp.50–1	*Teacher's Book* 3, pp.58–73
	Unit 4: Rocks and soils • Hard rocks pp.58–9 • Testing soils pp.62–3 • Soil and water pp.64–5	*Teacher's Book* 3, pp.74–89
	Unit 5: Magnets and springs • Strength of magnets pp.72–3 • Stretching and squeezing pp.74–5 • Exploring springs pp.76–7 • Spring power pp.78–9	*Teacher's Book* 3, pp.90–105
	Unit 6: Friction • Measuring forces pp.84–5 • Slippery surfaces pp.86–7 • Exploring friction pp.92–3	*Teacher's Book* 3, pp.106–121
Present results in drawings, bar charts and tables.	Unit 1: Living and growing • Food types pp.6–7 • Clean teeth pp.20–1	*Teacher's Book* 3, pp.16–38
	Unit 2: Helping plants grow well • Growing plants pp.26–7 • Plants and water pp.30–1	*Teacher's Book* 3, pp.40–57
	Unit 3: Characteristics of materials Building bridges pp.44–5 • Exploring paper pp.48–9	*Teacher's Book* 3, pp.58–73
	Unit 4: Rocks and soils • Hard rocks pp.58–9 • Soil and water pp.64–5	*Teacher's Book* 3, pp.74–89
	Unit 5: Magnets and springs • Exploring springs pp.76–7 • Spring power pp.78–9	*Teacher's Book* 3, pp.90–105
	Unit 6: Friction • Measuring forces pp.84–5 • Slippery surfaces pp.86–7 • Testing spinners pp.90–1 • Exploring friction pp.92–3	*Teacher's Book* 3, pp.106–121
Scientific enquiry: Consider evidence and approach		
Draw conclusions from results and begin to use scientific knowledge to suggest explanations.	Unit 1: Living and growing • Clean teeth pp.20–1	*Teacher's Book* 3, pp.16–39
	Unit 2: Helping plants grow well • Growing plants pp.26–7 • Plants and water pp.30–1	*Teacher's Book* 3, pp.40–57
	Unit 3: Characteristics of materials • Building bridges pp.44–5 • Exploring paper pp.48–9 • Stretchy materials pp.50–1	*Teacher's Book* 3, pp.58–73

	Unit 4: Rocks and soils • Hard rocks pp.58–9 • Testing soils pp.62–3 • Soil and water pp.64–5	*Teacher's Book* 3, pp.74–89
	Unit 5: Magnets and springs • Magnetic materials pp.70–1 • Spring power pp.78–9	*Teacher's Book* 3, pp.90–105
	Unit 6: Friction • Slippery surfaces pp.86–7 • Different forces pp.88–9	*Teacher's Book* 3, pp.106–121
Make generalizations and begin to identify simple patterns in results.	Unit 3: Characteristics of materials • Stretchy materials pp.50–1	*Teacher's Book* 3, pp.58–73
	Unit 5: Magnets and springs • Exploring springs pp.76–7	*Teacher's Book* 3, pp.90–105

Biology

Biology: Plants

Know that plants have roots, leaves, stems and flowers.	Unit 2: Helping plants grow well • Roots and stems pp.28–9 • Plants and water pp.30–1 • Plants and light pp.32–3 • Plants and warmth pp.34–5	*Teacher's Book* 3, pp.40–57 *Workbook* 3, pp. 17, 20
Explain observations that plants need water and light to grow.	Unit 2: Helping plants grow well • Plants and water pp.30–1 • Plants and light pp.32–3	*Teacher's Book* 3, pp.40–57 *Workbook* 3, p.20
Know that water is taken in through the roots and transported through the stem.	Unit 2: Helping plants grow well • Roots and stems pp.28–9 • Plants and water pp.30–1	*Teacher's Book* 3, pp.40–57
Know that plants need healthy roots, leaves and stems to grow well.	Unit 2: Helping plants grow well • Growing plants pp.26–7 • Roots and stems pp.28–9 • Plants and water pp.30–1 • Plants and light pp.32–3 • Plants and warmth pp.34–5	*Teacher's Book* 3, pp.40–57 *Workbook* 3, pp.14,15,17
Know that plant growth is affected by temperature.	Unit 2: Helping plants grow well • Plants and warmth pp.34–5	*Teacher's Book* 3, pp.40–57 *Workbook* 3, p.22

Biology: Humans and animals

Know life processes common to humans and animals include nutrition (water and food), movement, growth and reproduction.	Unit 1: Living and growing • I'm special pp.2–3 • My wonderful senses pp.4–5 • Food types pp.6–7	*Teacher's Book* 3, pp.16–39 *Workbook* 3, pp.5–7
Describe differences between living and non-living things using knowledge of life processes.	Unit 2: Helping plants grow well • Sorting plants into groups pp.24–5	*Teacher's Book* 3, pp.40–57
Explore and research exercise and the adequate, varied diet needed to keep healthy.	Unit 1: Living and growing • Healthy eating pp.8–9 • Keeping active pp.10–11 • A question of balance pp.12–13	*Teacher's Book* 3, pp.16–39 *Workbook* 3, pp.2,3,6
Know that some foods can be damaging to health, e.g. very sweet and fatty foods.	Unit 1: Living and growing • Healthy eating pp.8–9 • A question of balance pp.12–13 • Healthy teeth pp.18–19	*Teacher's Book* 3, pp.16–39 *Workbook* 3, pp.2,6
Explore human senses and the ways we use them to learn about our world.	Unit 1: Living and growing • My wonderful senses pp.4–5	*Teacher's Book* 3, pp.16–39 *Workbook* 3, p.1

13

Sort living things into groups, using simple features and describe rationale for groupings.	Unit 1: Living and growing • Food types pp.6–7 Unit 2: Helping plants grow well • Sorting plants into groups pp.24–5	*Teacher's Book* 3, pp.16–39 *Teacher's Book* 3, pp.40–57

Chemistry

Chemistry: Material properties

Know that every material has specific properties, e.g. hard, soft, shiny.	Unit 3: Characteristics of materials • Different materials pp.40–1 • Using materials pp.42–3 • Comparing materials pp.46–7 Unit 4: Rocks and soils • Hard rocks pp.58–9	*Teacher's Book* 3, pp.58–73 *Workbook* 3, pp.23–5 *Teacher's Book* 3, pp.74–89 *Workbook* 3, pp.40,41
Sort materials according to their properties.	Unit 3: Characteristics of materials • Different materials pp.40–1 • Using materials pp.42–3 Unit 4: Rocks and soils • Hard rocks pp.58–9	*Teacher's Book* 3, pp.58–73 *Workbook* 3, pp.23–4 *Teacher's Book* 3, pp.74–89 *Workbook* 3, pp.38–9
Explore how some materials are magnetic but many are not.	Unit 5: Magnets and springs • Magnetic forces pp.68–9 • Magnetic materials pp.70–1	*Teacher's Book* 3, pp.90–105 *Workbook* 3, pp.51–4
Discuss why materials are chosen for specific purposes on the basis of their properties.	Unit 3: Characteristics of materials • Different materials pp.40–1 • Using materials pp.42–3	*Teacher's Book* 3, pp.58–73 *Workbook* 3, pp.23–5

Physics

Physics: Forces and motion

Know that pushes and pulls are examples of forces and that they can be measured with forcemeters.	Unit 5: Magnets and springs • Magnetic forces pp.68–9 • Stretching and squeezing pp.74–5 Unit 6: Friction • Measuring forces pp.84–5	*Teacher's Book* 3, pp.90–105 *Workbook* 3, pp.57 *Teacher's Book* 3, pp.106–121 *Workbook* 3, pp.67–8
Explore how forces can make objects start or stop moving.	Unit 6: Friction • What is friction? pp.82–3 • Measuring forces pp.84–5 • Slippery surfaces pp.86–7	*Teacher's Book* 3, pp.106–121 *Workbook* 3, p.71
Explore how forces can change the shape of objects.	Unit 5: Magnets and springs • Stretching and squeezing pp.74–5	*Teacher's Book* 3, pp.90–105
Explore how forces, including friction, can make objects move faster or slower or change direction.	Unit 6: Friction • What is friction? pp.82–3 • Measuring forces pp.84–5 • Slippery surfaces pp.86–7 • Different forces pp.88–9	*Teacher's Book* 3, pp.106–121 *Workbook* 3, pp.66,75

Resources for *Heinemann Explore Science* Grade 3

Science equipment and durable items

balance scale
cold-water paste
digital balance
digital camera or a video camera with a timer
digital microscope
floor vinyl
forcemeter
hand lens or magnifying glass
light sensor
magnetic and non-magnetic metals
magnets

masses, up to and including 500g
measuring jug or cylinder
measuring stick or tape measure
metal samples
metre ruler
models of teeth or real teeth (milk and adult)
newtonmeter
OHP transparencies
pH indicator strips
plank or ramp
rocks and minerals reference books and field guides

sieves with different-sized holes
simple watering systems
small beakers or glasses
small mirrors
spinner template
stopwatch or other seconds timer
strips of metal
strips of plastic
strips of wood
video camera
weighing scales
whiteboard
wooden block and pieces of wood

Consumables and items locally available

backing/display paper
beads with large holes
blotting paper
bricks (to support end of a plank)
bubble wrap
card
cardboard
carpet
carrier bags
chocolate
clay
clear glass jars
cork
cotton reels
cotton wool
cress seeds
different soils or sand, clay, peat and compost mixtures
disclosing tablets
dog food and hamster mix (including tins, pictures, etc.).
elastic bands
examples of all the food groups as pictures
felt
filter paper
fizzy drinks
foil
food colouring
funnels or the tops of pop bottles

graph paper
hoops
ink
J-cloth
kitchen scales (operated with a spring)
knives
leather bags
liquid soap
long tube or plastic pop bottle with the top cut off
marbles or small masses (e.g. coins)
matchsticks
mouthwash
paper
paper bags
paper clips
paper spiral
paper towel
permanent marker pen
pictures of different plants
pictures of the students as babies
plastic bags
plastic tub
plasticine
plates
pop bottles
pot plants
rocks

sand
sandpaper
saucers
skulls or diagrams of different animals
small plant pots
socks in different thicknesses, colours and sizes
soft cloth
spent matchsticks or craft matchsticks
spoons
steel paper clips
sticky tape
string
sweet jars
tea-stained mugs
toothbrushes
toothpaste
toy cars
turfs of grass
variety of fruit and vegetables
vegetable oil
very small pots
wallpaper paste or clear liquid soap
water
water-filled measuring cylinder

Unit 1: Living and growing

The objectives for this Unit are that students should be able to:

- Understand how they grow up to be healthy
- Know what a balanced diet consists of
- Plan nutritious meals to meet their body's needs
- Learn how they use their teeth and how to keep them healthy.

SB p.1   Science background

We are all unique. Humans, like other animals, eat, move, grow and reproduce. Because animals, unlike plants, are unable to make their own food, they have to eat to live and grow.

Generally, foods can be divided into providers of energy or growth. They include carbohydrates, fats, protein, vitamins and minerals. Carbohydrates are found in bread, pasta, rice and cereals as starches. They are found in biscuits, cakes and sweets as sugars. Both provide energy, but sugars can do more harm to the teeth than starches. Athletes eat a lot of starchy foods for energy.

Other essential foods include water, and minerals like sodium and fibre. Our bodies are 70 per cent water! If we lose just 1 per cent of that, we will feel thirsty and need to drink. Sodium is only required in small amounts. Most comes naturally in food, but we add more in the form of sodium chloride (table salt). Too much salt can cause high blood pressure. Fibre is used to move our food through our gut. There is plenty in grains, cereals, fruit and vegetables.

Students need to be aware that different foods belong to different groups and that these groups provide us with different requirements.

Our milk teeth need to be healthy as they grow before the permanent teeth. The first permanent molar usually erupts when a child is about 6 years old, but is often missed as it is far back in the mouth. Like all teeth, this must be cared for properly.

Proper chewing is important as this helps to guide the new teeth into the correct position. To keep teeth healthy, we need to drink plenty of water, brush after meals, floss between them and eat fresh fruit and vegetables. Our teeth are mainly calcium, so drinking plenty of calcium-rich milk when young will help their development. Healthy gums also are essential for healthy teeth.

Language

Bacteria	Single-celled organisms found everywhere.
Diet	A control of what is eaten for health, not just to lose weight.
Nutrition	The act or process of eating and using the nutrients in food for living and growing.
Carbohydrate	Provides the body with energy. Found in bread, rice, pasta, potatoes and sugar.
Minerals	Simple substances found naturally. Help to build the body and keep it healthy.
Plaque	A build-up of bacteria on the teeth that can be scraped off by a dentist or by brushing with a toothbrush.
Protein	Used for growth and repair of cells in the body. Found in meat, fish, pulses and nuts.
Vitamin	Chemical that the body needs to stay healthy.

The Words to learn list on page 1 of the *Student Book* can be used to make a classroom display.

Resources

- *Living and Growing* Reader.
- Pictures of the students as babies.
- Examples of all the food groups as pictures, packets or actual foods. Enough for each group of students to sort into food groups. Include beans, pulses and tofu.
- Skulls of different animals, or diagrams to show that carnivores have canines and herbivores do not. Herbivores have better-developed molars than carnivores.
- Models of teeth or sterilized real teeth (milk and adult).
- Small mirrors.
- Glasses and fizzy drinks.
- Digital camera or microscope and computer.
- Hand lenses.
- Secondary sources for dog food and hamster mix (including tins, pictures, etc.).
- Toothpaste, toothbrushes and mouthwash.
- Tea-stained mugs.

- Light sensor.
- Rulers.
- Whiteboard.
- Disclosing tablets.

Bright ideas

- A digital camera or Intel microscope and computer can be used to monitor the decay of a tooth placed in a fizzy drink. Since the tooth can't be seen easily in cola, you could try using transparent lemonade, although there is less sugar in lemonade and decay will take longer. Students could compare the effects of the two drinks.

- In advance, set up a tooth in a sugary, fizzy drink so students can see what happens after a week and after several weeks. The results are quite conclusive!

- Eggshell is a thin version of a tooth if you can't get hold of real teeth. (A whole egg in vinegar goes rubbery in about 3 days as the shell dissolves, leaving the membrane behind.) Try asking your local dentist for sterilized teeth.

Knowledge check

- Students should be aware that what they eat is important.
- Students should be aware that we need exercise to stay healthy.
- Students should know that different animals and people eat different diets.
- Students may be aware that they should brush their teeth at least twice a day.
- Most students will have visited the dentist and some may have seen relatives or older friends with braces fitted by the orthodontist.

Skills check

Students need to:
- decide what evidence and measurements they want to take
- collect evidence and decide how good it is
- communicate their findings to others.

Some students will:
- present their evidence in drawings, bar charts and tables.

Links to other subjects

Literacy:	Writing simple non-chronological reports from known information. Writing for a known audience (e.g. other students). Comparing the way information is presented.
Numeracy:	Organizing and interpreting simple data in tables, e.g. list of foods eaten being organized into a table and graphs.
Information Communication Technology (ICT):	Using a digital microscope and digital camera. Using PowerPoint to produce a presentation.
Personal, Social and Health Education (PSHE):	Developing a healthy, safe lifestyle, including healthy eating such as planning a healthy meal, and knowing why we brush our teeth, e.g. to remove the bacteria that cause plaque. Recognizing the value of our senses and how those who have lost one or more senses cope.
Geography:	Learning about other cultures and their eating restrictions, e.g. Hindus do not eat beef products as cows are sacred.
History:	Becoming aware of different ways of life at different times in history, e.g. what diets were like, why people often had bad teeth and what they used to clean their teeth.

Let's find out...

The Unit opens with this question:

Your teeth are special! When you visit the dentist, she looks at your teeth to see if they are healthy. Why does she want you to clean your teeth after every meal? Why might she ask you to floss between your teeth? What else can you do to keep your teeth healthy?

Discuss the problem. Encourage the students to make suggestions or predictions. Note any misconceptions and probe to find out why they believe what they say. Tell them they are going to learn about what we need to eat to be healthy and how to keep our teeth clean.

17

Unit 1: Living and growing – I'm special

The objectives for this lesson are that students should be able to:

- Learn that all animals grow in the same way
- Understand that all animals need food and water
- Research and record how animals grow and change
- Discover how twins are made.

SB pp.2–3

Starter

- Use photographs of the students as they are now to point out that each one is unique. Every single one can be recognized from their picture. They are all different, and they are all special.
- Choose one student, perhaps not known to them, and talk about them in particular. It might be a student known to you, and you may be able to show photographs of them at different stages in their life. How are they different from the students in your class? How are they the same?

Explain

New you

It may be appropriate to ask the students to begin to write and illustrate a brief autobiography. If the class is new to you, this may help you to learn more about your new students. Be careful with personal and confidential information. Emphasize that each of us is unique and very special. Emphasize the parenting role.

Animals need food and water

Because animals are unable to make their own food as plants can, they need to move to find it. So animals need to be aware of their surroundings and this has led to the development of their senses. Young, helpless animals are fed by their parents until they can find food for themselves.

Growing and changing

Students can confuse growing with swelling up. Growing is adding material to yourself. Along with growth, animals, including humans, change. Ask the students to think of all the things they can do now that they could not do when they were helpless babies. This activity is greatly enhanced if you know a parent who will bring a newborn or young baby into class for comparisons.

Things to do

How are you growing and changing?

Students will be engaged by making comparisons between themselves as babies and as they are today. They might compare all kinds of information, including height, weight, hair colour, and all kinds of skills. Focus on teeth, both milk and adult, and the importance of taking care of them.

Record

Students can mount and annotate pictures of themselves to show how they have changed. Pictures could be scanned and printed for this exercise.

Support

Some students may be unable to provide information on their early childhood or it may be inappropriate for them to share it with others. Be sensitive to this and be prepared to provide pictures cut from catalogues or magazines to allow them to compare the changes that take place as we grow and change.

Extend

A visit from someone in one of the caring professions would enhance this activity. This will be helped enormously if the students prepare questions for them in advance.

Dig deeper

Students have the opportunity to find out more about animal young and how young mammals are fed.

Did you know?

In the Linnaean classification system, humans are part of the animal kingdom along with other mammals such as apes, cattle and horses. Animals are distinguished from plants by independent movement and responsive sense organs.

18

- You may have twins or other multiple birth children in your class. Some twins are identical of course, while others are not. Identical twins result from the splitting of a fertilized egg early in the pregnancy, while non-identical twins are the product of two different fertilizations, which is why it is possible to have twins of each sex. Be sensitive to whether your twins want attention drawn to them.

- Figures vary, but something like 70–75 per cent of the human body is water. This water is constantly being lost, which is why it is important to both drink water and eat foods that contain it.

- The Jerboa is a small nocturnal rodent, native to the deserts of Africa and Asia. Adapted for desert living, it gets all its water from its diet of plants, seeds and insects, and does not need to drink, unlike most other animals.

I wonder...

Identical and non-identical twins are explained in Did you know? Identical twins share 100 per cent of the same human DNA, but two brothers or sisters will share 99.95 per cent and even two unrelated humans share 99.9 per cent. You might discuss nature and nurture, how much we are a product of our parents, and how much we are affected by surroundings. While some identical twins celebrate their similarities, others look for and emphasize differences between them.

Other ideas

Animal parenting

There is a relationship between parenting and the number of offspring that animals produce. If parental care is non-existent, for example when fish or invertebrate animals lay eggs and simply leave them, the chances of these new animals surviving to maturity is extremely small. Large numbers of eggs are laid in this situation. When parental care is strong, as for example in many of the vertebrates, there are fewer young, but the commitment and the survival rate is far greater. Penguins, for example, only lay one egg at a time, and care for their chick with great effort and patience. Students could explore this by finding out how many eggs different animals lay and how long they are cared for by their parents.

There is a relationship, too, between the place where an animal is born and its speed of maturing. Animals born in holes and burrows, where they are protected to some extent from predators, are often born very immature, blind and helpless. Animals born in exposed places, such as open plains and hillsides, are born mature. For example, a newborn foal is quickly on its feet and able to run from predators. Again, students may like to explore how true this is of animals they know.

Presentation

Where appropriate, students may like to present something about themselves, their families and friends, to the rest of the class or school, celebrating their uniqueness.

At home

Parental involvement in these activities is important and it may be appropriate to send a letter home in advance, explaining that the students will be looking at their own early years.

Plenary

You might finish this Unit by introducing examples of famous people who have been, or are, unique because of overcoming disabilities and disadvantages.

19

Unit 1: Living and growing – My wonderful senses

The objectives for this lesson are that students should be able to:

- Learn that humans have five different senses
- Understand that not everyone likes the same tastes, smells, etc.
- Make a sensory map of the school
- Imagine how it would feel to have impaired senses.

SB pp.4–5

Starter

- Bring a delicious-smelling and tasting food into the classroom – warm bread or cakes are ideal. Make sure you have checked for any allergies first and, if required by your school, send a letter home as tasting will be involved here.
- Ask the children to smell the bread. *How does it smell?* Look carefully at it. *How does it look? Let's eat some!* Give out the cut slices and ask children to use all of their senses to describe the food.

⚠️ Check for allergies – a letter should be sent home if testing foods.

Explain

Five fabulous senses

Explain that humans have five fabulous senses that help us to find out about the world around us. Children are likely to have covered senses in Kindergarten so remind them of what they know. Link the sense to the sense organ. We see with our... eyes, we hear with our... ears, etc. Ask the children to describe some of their favourite smells, sounds and tastes. What smells, sounds and tastes do they dislike?

Very receptive

The receptors of the different sense organs are made to respond to different things. Receptors in the ears respond to sounds, but other receptors also respond to movement so help you keep your balance. The tongue has receptors that respond to substances in food. Your skin responds to touch, temperature, pressure and pain, and your nose has receptors inside it which respond to chemicals in the air that we recognize as smells. Nerve cells in the receptors carry messages to your brain, which processes the information and recognizes the sensations.

Sight and hearing

If you have hearing- or sight-impaired children in the class, you may need to be particularly sensitive when discussing blindness or deafness. Ask students to imagine what it might be like to have lost one of their senses. Be positive and introduce the stories of role models with sight impairment such as Andrea Bocelli the opera singer and Stevie Wonder the singer, or from history Admiral Lord Nelson, Eduard Degas and Claude Monet. Esref Armagan is a famous Turkish artist, who is blind, and the former Indonesian President Abdurrahman Wahid had severe sight loss. Nelson Mandela and Kate Adie, the BBC World Service presenter, both have hearing loss.

Things to do

Using your senses

Make a sensory map of your school and grounds. Students will need to make close observations as they stop at particular points around the school to take photographs or recordings, and to use their senses to get a sensory picture of the location. In the classroom, work collectively to make a sensory collage of the area.

⚠️ Students must not taste things they find around the school.

Record

Students can mount and annotate pictures of different areas of the school and make texture rubbings of interesting things around them that stimulate the sense of touch. Make recordings for playback using mini digital recorders.

Support

Some students may be unable to participate because of sensory impairment they themselves have. Encourage them to focus on the senses they feel most comfortable with.

Extend

A visit from someone in one of the support professions or charities working with the sensory impaired would enhance this activity. This will be helped enormously if the students prepare questions in advance.

Dig deeper

Students have the opportunity to find out more about sign language and Braille.

Did you know?

- Police in Europe have used bloodhounds to help them track missing people or criminals since the 18th century. Today we use dogs to detect illegal drugs, explosives and weapons and also to help find people trapped after earthquakes or natural disasters.

- A good sense of hearing is vital for survival for most animals. Although the grasshopper does not have external ears like we do, it has a sense organ for hearing called the tympanum, which is located behind its legs.

- Newborn babies can only see about 30 cm (12 inches) in front of them clearly – just enough to see the person holding them. As they grow older, their binocular vision develops and they can focus on moving objects and have colour vision. By five or six months they can see as well as we can.

I wonder…

Like many animals, bats are born blind but quickly develop vision. In fact many bats can see perfectly well. However, they navigate and find prey with a unique system called echo location, where they make very high-pitched sounds that bounce back to them off objects in their path and help them to recognize objects and where they are. There is evidence that they can identify texture and shape.

Other ideas

WS 1

My wonderful senses

The students write a senses poem to describe your school using WS 1.

Fooling our senses

Most people use all of their senses in conjunction to get a picture of what the world is like. If we isolate senses, we sometimes find it far more difficult to recognize familiar things. Try putting an object into a cloth bag with drawstrings and asking a student to describe it using only the sense of touch – the others should try to guess what it is from the description.

The food we eat and our enjoyment of it is influenced by how it looks. Try making a selection of flavoured jellies but add black food colouring to them. Allow the students to taste the different jellies. Can they identify the flavour from the taste alone or do they need the colour cue? Compare with normal coloured jelly. Use vegetarian jelly, or ensure that you have checked the origin of the gelatin if it is from an animal source.

Presentation

Encourage students to present their research findings about Braille, sign language or a blind or hearing-impaired figure, from history or the present day, to the rest of the class in the form of a short documentary film or biographical entry for an encyclopaedia.

At home

Parental involvement in these activities is important and it may be appropriate to send a letter home in advance, explaining that the students will be looking at senses and tasting foods.

Plenary

You might finish this Unit by learning a song in sign language! Use a website for the hearing impaired.

New International Edition

Unit 1: Living and growing – Food types

The objectives for this lesson are that students should be able to:

- Identify and group different types of food

- Understand that animals, including humans, need food and water to stay alive, grow and be active

- State that they need a healthy diet to live and to grow

- Make a pictorial record of their diet.

SB pp.6–7

Starter

- Show photographs of young animals. *How does a baby animal grow to be an adult?* Continue with questions on the type of food they might eat and the quantity.

- Bring in some foods a baby animal might eat and discuss what foods they move on to. Most babies have liquid food and then learn to eat solids. A mother's milk provides some immunity for the baby as well as being a nutritious tailor-made food. You could bring in some jars of baby food for the students to try.

> ⚠ Check for allergies – a letter should be sent home if tasting foods.

Explain

Growing up

Discuss what the students ate for dinner last night. What are the students' food likes and dislikes? Why are they persuaded to eat their 'greens' or the crusts on their bread?

Where do you get your energy?

Ask questions on where we get the energy to run, move and play games. Most students will know it is food, but not which kinds. Ask what they think famous athletes and footballers eat or don't eat. Ask students how they might feel after spending a day running around. They should feel hungry!

Carbohydrates and fats provide us with the energy to be active. In extreme conditions we have to utilize our proteins, too – which is why starving people lose so much body weight.

What should you eat?

Bring in a range of foods. Ask students to sort them, or to say which foods an athlete would eat from the foods present. Discuss what each food group provides us with. Explain that the process of eating and drinking enough for our needs and how our bodies use food and drink to keep us healthy is called nutrition. Foods that are good for us and keep us healthy are called 'nutritious'. Introduce a ready meal or a mixture of foods, e.g. curry and rice, and ask the students if they can decide which group it belongs to. It should be broken down to give groups of protein and carbohydrate.

Things to do

Putting food into groups

Leave the foods from before in groups with labels. This will help the students to put their own foods into groups. This is fun if the students draw their meals on three plates, attach them to a piece of paper and then add the labels.

Record

Writing lists or drawing pictures of the kinds of food that are common in each food group will help students to remember them.

Support

If students have forgotten what they ate yesterday, ask them instead to write down their favourite foods for the three meals in a day. Let students use different colours to underline a list of the foods that they eat to indicate those that give energy and those that provide growth.

Extend

Ask students to plan a healthy but tempting meal that someone their age would want to eat, and make a table of the different food groups.

Did you know?

This reminds students of the importance of Vitamin C, and of the sheer quantity of food that they will eat in a lifetime. Other interesting facts include:

- People who regularly start each day eating a bowl of cold breakfast cereal with milk tend to consume more fibre and calcium, but less fat, than people who breakfast on other foods.

- Rice is the staple food of more than one-half of the world's population. Rice alone does not provide a balanced diet.

I wonder...

Unless you had tomato, lettuce and salad with the burger, the meal would be short on vitamins and minerals. The burger contains protein and there is carbohydrate in the bun. The cheese contains protein and also fat. Calcium in the cheese is needed for healthy teeth and bones. The fries have carbohydrate and fat from being deep-fried.

The apple pie is mainly sugar (carbohydrate); the small amount of vitamins is destroyed by cooking the apples. Every food group is present, but it isn't a balanced meal as there is far more carbohydrate and fat than anything else.

Other ideas
WS 2

Choosing a meal

Complete WS 2. As an extension task, allocate each student a food from the list in WS 2 and ask them to organize themselves into groups to match the five main food groups. They will find that some of them need to be in two groups. They should stand in the group they think the food provides most of. Discuss the groups. From these groups the students should sort themselves into meals that are balanced. Write down the meals, labelling the group to which each food belongs.

Good enough to eat

Set a design and technology task to produce a food packet for a healthy food that they don't really like. Can they make it look good enough to eat?

Presentation

Create a 'Healthy but delicious!' poster display using the food packets the students have designed. Ask the students to pretend that they are food specialists. They are to give a presentation of their poster, making the healthy food they chose sound delicious. The class could vote on their favourite meal.

At home
WS 3

Ask students to write down all the food groups they eat at home in one week. They can use WS 3 to record this in a simple bar chart.

Plenary

Discuss with students why they need to eat foods containing protein and carbohydrate. What would happen to them if they didn't have them? They should recognize that they need protein to grow and carbohydrate to give them energy to move.

Unit 1: Living and growing – Healthy eating

The objectives for this lesson are that students should be able to:

- Learn that humans need a variety of foods in their diets to stay healthy

- Understand that people from different cultures eat different foods

- Plan and present a healthy meal for a vegetarian

- Discover that food needs to be prepared and stored carefully.

SB pp.8–9

Starter

- Show a picture of healthy food. Discuss why this food would be healthy. *Is any food group missing?* Talk about vegetarians supplementing their diet with nuts, pulses and beans to gain the protein that they are not having from meat. Often their diet will be healthier than a meat-eater's because they eat no animal fat.

- Show pictures of dishes from different cultures. Ask students if these meals are balanced. They will need to look carefully at the items on the plates.

- After checking on food allergies, provide students with samples of tofu or vegetarian food, without telling them that they are meatless. *Is this meat?* This will show that vegetarians can still have a varied diet without meat. Provide examples of soy milk and other soy products too.

⚠️ Hygiene in giving out food – make sure students wash their hands before and after handling food. Check for allergies and cultural diferences – a letter should be sent home if you are to be tasting foods.

Explain

The same, but different

Discuss foods that seem very different from a taste point of view, but are examples of the same food groups.

An apple a day...

Bring in some fruit, including some unusual ones. Discuss which food group they belong to. If you eat a lot of fruit and vegetables (you should eat at least five portions every day), then you should be healthy. If you eat far too much fruit, and little else, it will force your food through your guts very quickly, resulting in diarrhoea!

Too much and too little

Be cautious here as students may already be sensitive about body image. Eating disorders are becoming more common and students will be aware of 'dieting' due to media coverage. Students at this age should not be trying to lose weight, unless they have been medically instructed to do so. They should be encouraged to eat a healthy and varied diet. They are still growing and are most active at this age, so should eat and drink plenty. The ideal is to cut down on fatty and sugary foods.

Things to do

Healthy diets

True vegetarians cut out meat and fish; a vegan eliminates any product that exploits an animal. They will not eat cheese, eggs, dairy produce, honey, meat or fish. Some refuse to wear anything that comes from an animal, e.g. leather or wool.

Record

In groups, encourage students to create a menu for a vegetarian restaurant from their planned meals. They could use word-processing and drawing software to design and illustrate the menus.

Support

Some students might need help to ensure that there is plenty of protein in the vegetarian diet. Give them a list of possible foods to use.

Extend

Ask students to plan a healthy diet for a vegan. Legumes (e.g. beans, peas, lentils and peanuts)

24

are excellent sources of protein and fibre. Fortified orange juice and figs provide calcium. Often vegan/vegetarian foods are manufactured to look like their meat counterparts! This activity will test students and encourage them to use their imaginations to provide a healthy diet.

Dig deeper

Students have the opportunity to find out more about healthy and unhealthy foods.

Did you know?

The first fact illustrates that food preservation was a key issue long ago, as well as today. The second shows that a varied menu is needed for a healthy diet.

- The largest item on any menu in the world is probably roast camel, sometimes served at wedding feasts. The camel is stuffed with a sheep's carcass, stuffed with chickens, which are stuffed with fish, which are stuffed in turn with eggs.

I wonder...

The chicken eats corn, which is a grain from a plant. The rice is a grain from another plant and the naan bread is made from flour, which is ground wheat – a grain from a third type of plant.

Other ideas

Food hygiene

Explain the importance of putting food away in the right place. Meat and dairy products are kept in the fridge or freezer to stop bacteria multiplying and making the food go off. Vegetables are kept in cool places (cupboards or the salad drawer of the fridge). Canned or dried food in packets has already been preserved by removing the air or water, so can be stored in cupboards.

- Discuss how fresh foods were stored before electricity, e.g. in larders, cellars or ice houses.

What is a diet?

Students could look this word up in a dictionary or encyclopaedia.

Other cultures

Plan a meal for students from another ethnic group that fits their dietary laws.

Presentation

Create a restaurant display using the menus and food group plates the students created previously.

Encourage students to make a PowerPoint presentation to illustrate foods that can be used to supplement a meat-free diet with protein.

At home

WS 4

Find out how long foods can be kept in the fridge or freezer. Freezers have a star system (one star per month). All foods must display a 'use by' or 'best before' date.

Ask students to complete WS 4. They must decide where to store each food item.

Plenary

Play a quiz game. Show some foods, or pictures of foods, and ask questions. Where shall I keep it? Would a vegetarian eat it? Would a Hindu? Include some less familiar dishes.

Unit 1: Living and growing – Keeping active

The objectives for this lesson are that students should be able to:

- Learn that exercise is important for a healthy lifestyle

- Discover how people can become more healthy

- Understand what aerobic exercise is

- Participate in regular exercise routines in the classroom or school.

SB pp.10–11   *Starter*

- Jog into the classroom in full gym gear – vest, shorts, trainers, headband and sweat bands – if appropriate. Exaggerate your exhaustion and huff and puff. Talk about how you've been thinking about your lifestyle and have decided to try to get a bit fitter. However, you're finding going to the gym a bit difficult to fit in with all of the other things you have to do.

- Explain that you're not really sure if exercise is doing you any good as now you're breathing harder, your heart is beating fast, and you just feel tired, hot and sweaty, and not fit. Can the students make any suggestions to help you get fitter and more healthy?

Explain

Getting moving

Discuss with the students what we mean by exercise and that any activity where you move your body is beneficial. Show pictures of sportspeople doing competitive sports such as swimming, basketball, gymnastics and football, and also show pictures of more mundane exercise such as doing housework, skipping, riding a bike, climbing stairs and dancing.

Staying strong

Some exercises are better for building strength – weightlifting, rowing, climbing and so on. These sorts of exercise can increase your muscles' size and efficiency.

A healthy heart

Ask the students if they know where their heart is. Explain that the heart is fairly central in their chest and leans slightly towards the left-hand side. It is about as big as their fist. Ask if the students know what the heart does. Explain how the heart is an important organ in the body as it pumps the blood around continuously every day of your life.

Now tell the students that they are going to do some exercise. Plan to do just 5 minutes of aerobic exercise with the class, such as running around the playground or doing star jumps. After the exercise period, ask the children how they feel. Can they feel their heart beating in their chest? What has happened to their breathing? Are they taking deeper, faster breaths? Do they feel warm?

Explain that exercise is good for your heart as it makes it work more and so get stronger. This sort of exercise is called aerobic as it encourages you to take in more oxygen. When you do aerobic exercise regularly, it helps your heart do its job better; that is, delivering oxygen in the form of oxygen-carrying blood cells to the rest of your body.

Explain that aerobic activities are the ones that leave you slightly out of breath and feeling warm.

Things to do

Lifestyle coach

Be cautious here as students may be self-conscious of their body image. Approach these issues with sensitivity and an understanding of cultural norms.

Ask the students to take on the role of Jalal's lifestyle coach. Explain that he sits in front of the television all day and never does any exercise. How can he increase his activity levels?

Elicit different forms of exercise and differentiate between aerobic and strength-building activities, although of course many forms of exercise are both. Also try to emphasize things that can be done without spending money such as walking rather than taking a bus or car, taking the stairs rather than a lift, skipping, jogging etc.

Discuss other things Jalal could do to become healthier and stress the need for exercise in conjunction with healthy eating. Don't forget the need for water! When we exercise, we sweat and that can lead to problems with dehydration – make sure that students have access to water throughout their exercise periods.

Record

In groups, students plan a 5-minute exercise routine that can be done in class or school. Each group in turn can act as aerobic coaches and teach the routine to the other groups. You might choose to have one group demonstrate their routine each day and film each one to use again.

Support

Some students may find exercise difficult so be sensitive to their needs and adapt routines to suit.

Extend

Ask students to research the diet and exercise regimes of famous athletes or sportspeople. *How are their diets and fitness schedules different from ours?* Extend by asking children to imagine what the sports stars would be like if they did not exercise but ate the same amounts of food. Most top athletes consume many more calories than the average person, but they do not become obese because they use up all of the energy from the food by exercising.

Did you know?

Some students might have asthma but this does not preclude their involvement in sport and exercise. Emphasize that exercise takes many forms and is not just participation in sports and competitive games. Small differences such as walking up stairs can make a difference to fitness levels.

I wonder...

It's almost impossible to say how much exercise is healthy and how much is too much. However, around an hour of physical activity on most days of the week for children and young people is considered adequate for good health.

Other ideas

Count your steps

Pedometers are devices that count the number of steps a person takes over the course of a day. If you have some of these, ask children to use them and count the numbers of steps taken in different activities or on different days of the week. What activity gets us moving the most?

Fitness week

Organize a whole-school fitness week and share your aerobic exercise routines with the rest of the school in assembly.

Presentation

Create an information leaflet for younger children on the benefits of a healthy lifestyle and suggest ways this can be achieved.

At home

WS 5

Make an exercise diary for a week. Encourage students to chart how much of their time is spent in activity that moves their bodies and how much is sedentary.

Plenary

Remind students that being fit is a way of saying that you eat a well-balanced and nutritious diet, get enough physical activity in your life and have a healthy weight. If you are fit, your body will work well and you'll feel good. Make a resolution, or promise, as a class to make a special effort to change one aspect of their lives this month to try to increase their fitness level – it could be as simple as walking for 20 minutes every day.

New International Edition

Unit 1: Living and growing – A question of balance

The objectives for this lesson are that students should be able to:

- Find out how to combine a balanced diet with enough exercise

- Research and record how to make their diet balanced and healthy

- Name some foods that provide energy and some that help us grow

- Learn how to do the best sort of exercise for them.

SB pp.12–13

Starter

Tell the story of a traveller who visited the five food islands. The first island she visited was the island of carbohydrates. 'Oooh,' she thought, 'my favourites – chips, potatoes, lovely bread. Yummy.' And she ate as much as she could. After a while she started to feel very, very full; full to bursting, bloated and not very well. 'Maybe the island of carbs isn't for me,' she thought.

Next she visited the island of fat and sugar where she gorged herself on biscuits, doughnuts, cakes and chocolates, which were great to begin with but soon her tummy began to feel a bit sick. 'I think I've had too many sweets,' she thought.

- Go on to describe the islands of fruit and vegetables, the meat and protein island and the isle of dairy. Students will quickly realize that no one food group can keep us healthy alone; we need food from all of the groups to have a balanced diet.

- Discuss with the students how even eating a balanced diet can't be guaranteed to keep us healthy – we need exercise too (as discussed in the previous lesson).

Explain

WS 6

Too much or not enough?

Be cautious when discussing weight issues with students and be sensitive to the feelings of students who may be struggling with weight issues themselves or have a poor body image. Emphasize the health benefits of a balanced diet rather than anything related to appearance. Discuss how eating too little can be just as damaging in the long term as eating too much.

Just right

WS6 presents the different food groups as a pie chart. As well as the different groups, this introduces approximate quantities, represented by the size of the pie 'slices'. Help students to understand and interpret this convention for presenting information.

Fantastic five

Emphasize that there are no really good or bad foods and that all food can be part of a healthy diet, as long as the balance is right. Current thinking suggests that carbohydrates and starchy foods form the basis of meals, with at least five portions of vegetables and fruits per day. We should be eating more fish and cutting down on sugar and fatty foods. We should also cut down on salt and drink more water, as well as becoming more active and maintaining a healthy weight.

Things to do

Balanced choices

Ask students to plan a day's food intake for Jalal and discuss the importance of having a good breakfast to start the day to help avoid snacking. Base meals on starchy carbohydrate foods with plenty of fruit and vegetables. Include lots of water in place of Jalal's favourite fizzy sodas.

Record

Encourage students to make a video postcard to send to Jalal with their suggestions on how to change his lifestyle for a healthier version.

Support

Some students may need additional reinforcement on food groups. Help them to make the food islands by decorating cardboard boxes with pictures of different foods from each group. Find pictures or photographs of a selection of foods and sort them into the relevant food groups. Each 'island' should contain several examples of food from each individual food group.

Extend

Students can begin some research on the contents of food as described in food labelling systems. Ask them to find out what information is displayed on food labels and what it means (nutritional values, calorific values, amount of salt, etc.). Does anything surprise them? Think of things such as sugar in baked beans or tomato ketchup, the amount of salt in a packet of crisps, etc.

Dig deeper

Students have the opportunity to find out more about balanced diets.

Did you know?

These facts illustrate to students that food has not always been the same as it is now and how we need food to live – even on the Moon. Exercise is revisited by looking at a typical walking speed.

I wonder...

This activity could be set for homework. Students could conduct a mini-survey among their classmates, friends and family as to which exercise they think is best for us. In class, compare results and construct a pictogram or bar chart of your combined results. Encourage students to give reasons for their choice of 'best' exercise.

Other ideas

Taste tests

⚠️ Check for allergies – a letter should be sent home if tasting foods.

Bring in some exotic or unfamiliar foods. Encourage students to try a taste of something new and different. Stress the importance of variety in a healthy diet so that eating becomes a pleasure not a chore.

Presentation

Ask students to present a television or magazine advert for a health and fitness spa. What are the key messages they need to include? What benefits should they stress?

At home

Ask students to canvass family and friends as to the exercise which is best for us as in the 'I wonder?' question.

Plenary

From the food island boxes you have made, ask a student to choose foods for a balanced meal, but miss out one of the food groups. Can the other students guess what food group is missing from the meal?

29

Unit 1: Living and growing – Animal food

The objectives for this lesson are that students should be able to:

- Find out that not all animals eat the same foods

- Tell the difference between animals based on what they eat

- Learn how to organize information into charts

- Recognize the difference between domesticated and wild animals and how they find food.

SB pp.14–15   *Starter*

- Show a picture of wolves and discuss what they eat. Bring in the word 'carnivore' to describe any animal that eats only meat. *Can you think of any other carnivores?*

- Show a picture of a panda. *What does this animal eat?* Explain that animals that eat only plants are called 'herbivores'. *Can you think of any other herbivores?*

- Some students may want to know how to classify humans as we eat both plants and meat. Discuss this and see if they can identify any other 'omnivores'.

Explain

Favourite foods

Discuss how different types of animal have developed different tools to help them eat the foods they like, e.g. giraffes' tongues, lions' claws.

Domesticated animals

Explain that domesticated animals are either carnivores or herbivores, just like the wild animals, and would have eaten similar foods. Bring in some dried pet foods and look at the ingredients on the packets to establish whether they contain meat.

Pet mice and gerbils still eat similar foods to their wild relatives, i.e. seeds and grains. Allow students to sort samples of the dried foods into piles. This will show the varied diet these food mixes provide, as they usually contain sunflower seeds, leaves, vegetables and corn.

Things to do   WS 7

Feeding time

Maya's notes are provided on WS 7. This activity encourages the students to think logically and to organize information into a manageable format.

Record

Encourage students to make a table, chart or pictogram using Maya's notes. As long as the record is clear and simple to follow, then Maya will be able to feed all the animals properly. Simple pictures are good; adding labels is even better. A clear graph to show quantities is the best way.

Support

Some students may think only in terms of writing the information out on one sheet of paper. Indicate that this will be more easily lost and they need something quick and easy to read, such as a picture of the animal and the food it eats.

Extend

Encourage students to produce a bar chart or pictorial guide that Maya could leave behind when she goes on holiday, which could direct other keepers on what to do. Students could begin to research food chains to learn more about what different animals eat.

Exploring

Students can use the Internet to begin to explore simple food chains – what eats what?

Did you know?

- Use these unusual facts to introduce and encourage discussion of animal diets.

I wonder…

This activity could be set for homework. In class, students can watch each other eat to see how their jaws move. Carnivores use their canines to tear large pieces of meat, so their jaws move 'up and down'. Herbivores use their incisors to 'snip' vegetation then chew with their molars, so their jaws move 'side to side' as they grind the food.

Other ideas

Fussy frogs

Schools that have kept tadpoles have tried feeding them tiny amounts of different foods, including proteins. The diet of tadpoles changes from plant to meat as they mature. If you fail to feed them meat, they will begin to eat each other.

Presentation

Ask students to draw a plan for a safari park so that the animals can live in large open areas. Remind them to think about which animals are carnivores and which are herbivores. Which animals can go in the same area? Which must be kept separate? Show the plans on a large wall display.

At home

Ask students to watch animals eating (domestic animals or animals on television) to find the answer to the 'I wonder' question.

Plenary

Ask each student to write 'carnivore' and 'herbivore' on separate pieces of paper. Say the names of animals and see if the students can hold up the correct description.

New International Edition

Unit 1: Living and growing – Types of teeth

The objectives for this lesson are that students should be able to:

- Learn that there are different types of teeth in their mouths

- Name and explain the four types of human teeth

- Understand the differences between human and animal teeth

- Find out what teeth are made of.

Starter

- If you have had a crown or other dental work done, you might have a cast of your mouth or teeth. Ask your dentist if he has any old models you can have. *What do you think this is? What do you notice about it?* If you can't get a cast, display a diagram of teeth in the jaw or use a large version of WS 8 to show different types of teeth.

- Ask students why we have teeth. *What would life be like without teeth? What would we eat? How would we talk? Do you have any relatives with false teeth?* Try talking with your lips pulled over your teeth to show how hard it would be without teeth.

Explain

How many teeth?

Discuss the different teeth, naming them and describing what they do. Students can look at each other's teeth to see the differences.

Teeth are our own cutlery!

We use our teeth to cut and tear our food as well as to hang on to it. In medieval times, when people used only their hands to eat, how did they make food the right size for their mouths? The knife was only used to carve large chunks from a piece of meat and then a mouth-sized piece was torn off with the teeth.

The Chinese only ever used knives in the kitchen to cut the meat into bite-sized pieces so it could be picked up with chopsticks. They considered it rude to use a knife at the table.

Strong handles are needed on cutlery. In the same way, healthy gums with a firm grip are needed to make our teeth effective.

Things to do

WS 8

Which job?

Students should mark and label the teeth they have on the mouth map diagram on WS 8. Use different foods to show what each type of tooth is used for. With crunchy foods, students should notice that they bite off a manageable piece with the incisors and then chew with the molars and premolars. Chewy foods show that the canines can be used to grip food. Emphasize the importance of healthy gums. Without a solid base, teeth cannot do their job correctly.

Record

Once students have labelled their teeth on the mouth map, they could make notes about which teeth do which job.

Support

Provide a list of characteristics to match up to the teeth, e.g. canines are pointed, molars have ridges.

Extend

Can students tell which of their teeth are permanent and which are still milk teeth? Milk teeth are smaller and generally have a more milky appearance than adult teeth.

Other animals' teeth

Look at the diagrams of teeth. Point out that the dog has larger canines to tear meat and that the sheep has more molars and no canines because it chews and grinds its food.

Record

Students should write a short sentence to say why each animal has particular teeth, e.g. the dog has large canines to grip and tear at meat. The sheep hasn't any canines as it doesn't eat meat.

Support

Some students will need help in identifying which teeth are which. Labelling teeth on the diagrams will help them draw conclusions.

Extend

Help students to look at a tooth under a microscope. Can they see the sharp edges on canines or ridges on molars?

Key ideas

The enamel part of the tooth is made from calcium. Since teeth are formed in our mouths before we are born, calcium is important in our diets. The enamel protects the nerves. Tooth decay becomes painful when nerves start to become exposed.

Did you know?

Vampire bats have sharp incisors to cut through skin, but as their diet is mainly liquid, they have less need for other types of teeth.

- Dogs have 42 teeth while cats have only about 30. Dogs are also more omnivorous than cats.
- The garden snail has around 14 175 teeth (105 rows, 135 teeth in each) on a long 'tongue' or radula.

I wonder...

The sugar content of the fizzy drink causes a build-up of plaque so the tooth will decay. Brushing will remove the acid and plaque. Demonstrate this to show the students how a rotten tooth looks and feels.

Other ideas

Rotting teeth

This is linked to the 'I wonder ...' question. Place a tooth in a glass of a sugary, fizzy drink and leave for a couple of weeks to see the effects. If you don't have a tooth, use a piece of eggshell. The shell is made of calcium so this works the same way, but faster. Set up an investigation using lemonade, cola and other fizzy drinks. A digital camera or the Intel microscope on time lapse can be used to observe the changes in the tooth over time.

Presentation

Ask the students to pretend that they are archaeologists who have found a new skull. They need to decide whether the animal was a carnivore or a herbivore and produce a presentation to explain.

Use papier mâché or plasticine to make models of different types of teeth. Arrange these on a wall display to create a 3-D mouth map.

At home

WS 9

Ask students to find out whether people at home have any fillings or any teeth missing. They should put the information into a table. This leads into the next lesson. The students could also mark which teeth have been removed or filled, using WS 9.

Plenary

Test the students' knowledge of the job each tooth does by asking them to write a short rhyme or ditty about it. Creating acrostics for each tooth type is also fun:

C   Can you see me?
A   At the corner of my smile
N   Next to the incisors
I   In front of the premolars
N   Not for chewing
E   Everyone knows I'm for gripping.

Unit 1: Living and growing – Healthy teeth

The objectives for this lesson are that students should be able to:

- Discover that humans have two sets of teeth

- Learn why they must look after their teeth

- Find out how to keep teeth healthy

- Plan and present an information leaflet using ICT.

SB pp.18–19 | **Starter**

- Start by asking the students if they have any teeth missing. *Do you think they will be replaced? What happens to the old teeth? Do you know what these first teeth are called? Can you guess why?*

- Explain why the first tooth falls out when the adult tooth pushes through. Discuss whether this happens all at once or gradually and whether all teeth come through as milk teeth first. The first molar, which usually appears when a child is about 6 years old, is a permanent tooth.

- Bad breath is often caused by poor dental hygiene. Try holding a cut onion or garlic near to students to see if they like the smell. Explain that brushing your teeth after eating foods with a strong smell will make your teeth clean and your breath smell better.

Explain

Growing teeth

Most students will have lost a few teeth by this age, or know friends who have. They should realize by now that without teeth we can't chew food. That's why baby animals have liquid foods, usually in the form of milk. This also provides calcium for the developing teeth (and bones). Even when babies start to have food other than milk, it is liquidized so that they can swallow it.

Students should realize that permanent teeth can't be replaced. If we lose one, we can't grow another

one, so there will be a gap. Dentists sometimes use caps, an implant or a bridge to fill gaps.

How long do we keep them?

Our adult teeth should last us a lifetime! Look at a picture of rotten teeth and discuss how we should look after our teeth. It might be useful to ask students to bring in their toothbrushes and show you how they brush their teeth. Otherwise, mime how to do it.

Things to do

Keeping teeth clean

This activity works particularly well after break or lunchtime because the students have just eaten. First check that disclosing tablets are permitted. The tablet is food dye and it dissolves into the mouth, coating all the plaque and bacteria in a stain. This rinses off with water. It is useful to ask students to bring a toothbrush to this lesson, so they can then clean their teeth afterwards! Students should identify the areas that are most stained (probably further back in the mouth). This means there are more bacteria in these areas, so we need to clean these teeth well too.

Explain to students that disclosing tablets are simply dye tablets. They can be safely chewed and sucked. This is not true of all tablets, e.g. medicines.

Record

Students can make a simple drawing of their teeth and what they see, and then write a description of how to remove the plaque.

Support

Make sure the students rub their tongues around their teeth, without swallowing the tablet! If they have cleaned their teeth recently, there might not be much stain.

Extend

Encourage students to think about what plaque is and how it might be formed.

Dig deeper

Students have the opportunity to find out which foods cause plaque to build up.

Did you know?

These facts should encourage students to look after their teeth.

- People don't always lose their teeth because of decay. The American singer Sheryl Crow has two false front teeth. Her own were knocked out when she tripped on a stage early in her career.

I wonder...

A milk tooth should have smaller roots and generally be a smaller tooth.

Other ideas

Brushing round corners

It is important that students know how to brush their teeth properly. Explain how to reach all the teeth by brushing them from top to bottom all the way round the mouth, including the molars.

Brush along the tops of the teeth and also on the insides, including behind the incisors. On any neglected teeth, bacteria will cause a build-up of plaque.

- Encourage students to think about how mouthwashes and flossing can help.

- Ask them to design a toothbrush to reach all the different places in the mouth and round the teeth to clean them easily. *What is the best shape?*

Presentation

Ask the students to pretend they are dentists and use word-processing software to write an information leaflet for other students, giving instructions on how to keep teeth clean and healthy. Print out the leaflets and display them.

Ask the students to design a package for a new toothpaste. It should look appealing, but also show all the benefits of using it.

At home

Ask students to check their toothpaste and write down the ingredients. *Which ingredient helps clean teeth? Which kills the bacteria?* Fluoride is used to strengthen teeth against decay, often included in drinking water. Baking soda is often used to help 'scrape' the stains from the teeth, especially in 'whitening' toothpaste.

Plenary

Ask students to suggest foods that are bad for teeth, e.g. sugary foods. *Which foods help to keep teeth healthy (e.g. fresh fruit and vegetables, milk, plenty of water)?* Discuss foods which have hidden sugars.

35

Unit 1: Living and growing – Clean teeth

The objectives for this lesson are that students should be able to:

- Find out the best way to clean their teeth
- Take part in a scientific investigation
- Make predictions on what their results will be
- Learn and try out different ways to display their findings.

Starter

SB pp.20–21

- Check students remember what they have learned about brushing their teeth. *What do we use to keep teeth clean? What kind of toothpaste do you use at home?*

- Show some different types of toothpaste and ask if there are any differences. People used to use tooth powder to scratch the stains from their teeth. Smokers whose teeth are stained yellow may use toothpastes like this.

- Bring in a toothbrush and some chocolate spread. Turn your back on the students and then turn round brushing your teeth with the chocolate mixture. Brush them properly, but then ask students why they are laughing (if they are!) or what you are doing wrong. They should know that you need proper toothpaste, not just anything on the brush!

The challenge

Read Which way is the best for cleaning your teeth? on page 20 in the *Student Book*. Toothpaste and brushing together are the best way to clean stains off the teeth. Explain what to do and discuss the different ways the groups carried out the experiment and collected their evidence. *Why were these good – or not so good – ideas?* Give each group of students an OHP transparency or sheet of clear plastic with 'stains' on it (coloured on with a black or brown permanent OHP pen). The ink must be permanent or it will rinse off with water.

What to do

The students should test the cleaning power of the techniques by:

- wiping the toothpaste onto the stain and then rinsing it off

- using a toothbrush with toothpaste on and rubbing it twice over the stain
- using a toothbrush with toothpaste on and rubbing it over ten times
- using the toothbrush without toothpaste and rubbing it over twice
- not doing anything (this will be the control).

The students should wash the toothpaste off the stain before testing how much light it lets through.

Just holding up a sheet to the light will not give quality results as it is a subjective comparison. Let students measure the amount of 'stain' removed by looking through the OHP sheet to view a piece of paper with a large word on it held by another student. The cleaner the OHP sheet, the further the student will be able to walk away before the word is no longer visible. The distance could be measured to give a quantitative reading of cleanliness.

Using a light sensor will produce even better quantitative results that can be interpreted. Take a test reading with the light sensor before you start the experiment to give a baseline measurement of how much light goes through the 'stain'. It is then possible to check how much of the 'stain' the students have removed.

The light sensor gives a reading in 'lux'. However, students at this stage are not expected to use these units so they have not been included in the table.

What you need

- toothbrushes
- toothpaste
- stained OHP transparencies or other clear plastic sheet
- permanent marker pen
- light sensor
- rulers

What to check

Students need to decide if one 'rub' is backwards and forwards, or in only one direction. They will also need to think about using a fair amount of toothpaste. Let them measure the amount coming out of the tube with a ruler.

Support

If students lose count of the number of rubs, encourage the whole group to count out loud. Some students may need help using the light sensor and interpreting the readings correctly. Remind students that each 'rub' should be of even pressure. They should test each technique on a part of the stain that hasn't already been rubbed.

Extend

Encourage students to think about whether the type of toothpaste used makes any difference.

What did you find?

WS 10

Ask students to record their measurements in the table on WS 10.

Record

Ask students to use their data to complete the bar chart on WS 10.

Present

Ask students to present their findings in groups. They could make a PowerPoint presentation and import images from the light sensor or digital camera to show what happened for each method. Set the slide transition to automatic to show what happened after each rub. The students should also include their table of results and charts. Can they tell the story of the chart and draw conclusions?

Can you do better?

WS 11

Ask students to review how good their evidence was. *Would you do anything differently if you were starting again? Is the evidence conclusive?* They haven't tested any different brands of toothpaste so they might ask if any particular brand is better.

Read Class 3's report on WS 11 together. *Did Class 3 draw the right conclusions from their results? What could they have done better?* Ask the students to comment on and criticize the report. This skill of evaluation is one of the hardest to teach and get right. If students learn at an early age to be constructively critical of their own and others' experiments, they will acquire a very important scientific skill. It can help to ask students to give their investigation a score out of ten. Ask them to justify their score. *Was the investigation really worth 9? Wasn't it better than 3?*

Now predict

Encourage students to give advice on how to make the method of testing fair, e.g. same pressure rubs, same toothpaste, etc.

Students should predict that the toothpaste that feels grittiest will be best at cleaning teeth.

Other ideas

Toothbrushes

Challenge students to find which of a number of toothbrushes cleans best by using them to clean the dirt from an old sieve. The best one will remove the dirt with ease and from all the corners. What can they find out about the types of bristle?

At home

Ask the students to carry out a survey to find out how often people clean their teeth and what toothpastes and mouthwashes they use. Encourage students to survey ten friends as the answers within one household are likely to be similar.

Plenary

Remind the students of the predictions they made before starting the investigation. Were they right? Show them a tea-stained mug. Explain that you've rinsed it, but it's still dirty. *What do you think we should do?* Encourage the students to apply what they have learned about cleaning teeth and realize that the best way would be to scrub the mug using detergent.

Unit 1: Living and growing – Unit 1: Review

The objectives for this lesson are that students should be able to:

- Check what they have learned about living and growing in this Unit

- Find out how they are working within the Grade 3 level.

SB p.22

Expectations

Students working towards Grade 3 level will:

- Recognize that we are all unique

- Recognize that all animals eat, move and reproduce

- Describe some of the types of food that they eat

- Recognize they need to take care of their teeth

- Recognize that there are different types of teeth

- Make observations and record these in tables.

In addition, students working within Grade 3 level will:

- Describe an adequate and varied diet for humans, recognizing that there are many ways of achieving this

- Explain how they should look after their teeth and recognize why they need to do so

- Name the four types of teeth and their functions

- Recognize that there should be something from each of the five food groups in a diet for it to be healthy

- Suggest questions about diet to be investigated

- Make relevant observations and present results in drawings, bar charts and tables

- Observe and compare teeth.

Further to this, students working beyond Grade 3 level will also:

- State that animals have different diets and may have different kinds of teeth

- Evaluate how strongly the evidence they have collected supports the conclusion they have drawn.

Check-up

Discuss the different ideas that Esher should write about.

- The diet sheet should contain at least one item from each food group in the main meal of the day, even if the other meals are not as well balanced. This means that, overall, the diet will be balanced.

- The instructions could be produced as part of an ICT project on a toothpaste package. They should include information on brushing properly and the importance of brushing regularly to avoid bad breath.

Assessment

WS 12

Use the Unit 1 assessment on WS 12 to check the students' understanding of the content of the Unit. The answers are given opposite.

Name: _____ Date: _____

WS 12 Unit 1 assessment

1 a) A baby doesn't eat the same food as you. Explain why.

_____

b) How many sets of teeth do we have?

_____

c) Name three things we must do to look after our teeth.

_____

2 Match the food group to its function in the human body.

Growth and repair of the body	Fat
Only used for energy	Vitamins/minerals
Needed for healthy development	Protein
Helps keep you warm	Carbohydrate

3 Different types of tooth do different jobs when we eat. What do these types of tooth do?

a) molar _____ b) incisor _____

4 Imran is testing what makes teeth decay. He puts one tooth into each drink for two weeks:

- Diet lemonade
- Tea with one sugar
- Tea with five sugars
- Cola

a) Predict which tooth will decay most. _____

b) Explain why. _____

Answers

1　a　A baby often doesn't have any teeth.

　　b　Two sets.

　　c　Any three of the following: brush regularly, use mouthwash, eat fruit and vegetables, drink water and milk, visit dentist.

2　Growth and repair of the body　　Fat

　　Only used for energy　　Vitamins/minerals

　　Needed for healthy development　　Protein

　　Helps keep you warm　　Carbohydrate

3　a　molar: chews and grinds food

　　b　incisor: cuts and snips food

4　a　The one containing the most sugar will decay most, i.e. the cola. Cola can have as much as 21 lumps of sugar per cupful.

　　b　Acids in many drinks dissolve tooth enamel. Plaque bacteria thrive on sugary foods. The more sugar, the faster the bacteria grow, so more plaque builds up. Plaque bacteria convert the sugar to acids, which also cause decay. That is why it is important to avoid too many sweet or acidic drinks, and to clean your teeth thoroughly.

The answer!

Refer back to the original question about the dentist. The students should now be able to explain that they should clean their teeth to kill bacteria so as to stop the build-up of plaque and keep their breath fresh. Flossing helps to remove food debris and bacteria from between the teeth and hard-to-reach areas. A visit from a dental professional would enable the students to show what they have learned. It would also allow them to confirm everything they have learned about using toothbrushes, toothpaste and mouthwash as well as eating food containing vitamins and minerals.

And finally...

Display the students' designs for toothpaste tubes, and the instructions on how to use them, to link with the meals they drew on plates to illustrate a healthy meal and a healthy lifestyle. Include printouts of slides from presentations, or even set the slide shows to run automatically. For open evenings or parents' evenings, this can be both educational and impressive.

New International Edition

Unit 2: Helping plants grow well

The objectives for this Unit are that students should be able to:

- Discover the differences between plants and animals
- Learn how plants grow
- Explain why humans need plants to survive
- Collect evidence and describe findings.

SB p.23   Science background

Plants are living things. They grow, change (slowly) and reproduce. Flowering plants reproduce with seeds. Flowers are pollinated by insects or by the wind.

Flowering plants range from the grasses to the tallest trees. Green plants make their own food by photosynthesis from the raw materials of water and carbon dioxide. For this to happen, their leaves need to catch the light of the Sun. Their whole structure is aimed at collecting and using as much sunlight as possible. They have a branching root system that can grip the soil; a stem (sometimes a trunk) that can hold the leaves up high and above the leaves of competitors; and a precise leaf pattern that ensures each leaf gets its bit of sunlight.

Leaves are the plant's food factories. They are also vital to our survival. Plants have produced most of the oxygen in the atmosphere. Every year, plants remove nearly 25 billion tonnes of carbon dioxide from the atmosphere, combining it with water to make living plant material. We use much of this living material as food – either by eating it directly or by eating the animals that eat the plants.

Plants will grow in the dark (most seeds germinate underground), but they are down to their food reserves if they have no sunlight. They grow long and spindly and lose their green colour. For healthy growth, plants need water, light and warmth (and a tiny quantity of mineral salts). By regulating these conditions, we can control plant growth.

Language

Branching key	Tool to identify something by a series of yes/no questions.
Flower	The reproductive part of a green plant.
Leaf	The plant's food factory. A leaf converts the energy in sunlight into chemical energy. This is stored in carbohydrates, which are produced within the leaf.
Root	The root anchors a plant and takes water and mineral salts from the soil.
Stem	The stem supports the leaves and flowers.
Germinate	When a seed starts to grow into a plant.

The Words to learn list on page 23 of the *Student Book* can be used to make a classroom display.

Resources

- *Helping Plants Grow Well* reader.
- Plants or pictures of different plants and two hoops.
- Pictures of four plants that can be sorted by yes/no questions.
- A variety of fruit and vegetables.
- Pot plants – start these from seed or buy them cheaply at the right time of the year. If you are growing plants from seed, start early and allow time for them to develop. Use broad beans in jam jars stuffed with crumpled paper towels to hold them at the sides. They need about 10 days to germinate and grow enough to use.
- Two turfs of grass – place in pots and place one in a dark place and one in the light. You could also do this with normal houseplants or cover some grass outside with black plastic sheeting or stones. Set this up about 10 days before you need it.
- Measuring tools – offer tapes, rulers and metre rules.
- Digital or video camera – make a photographic record to show growth as well as changes in the shape and orientation of a plant.
- Light sensor.
- Packets of small, easy to germinate seeds.
- Simple watering systems, e.g. very small pots.
- Saucers.

Bright ideas

- To prevent students losing interest long before a seed germinates or a bulb sprouts, accelerate the process with so-called 'fast plants', e.g. members of the cabbage family that have been bred to go through their whole life cycle in half a term. Look in science suppliers' catalogues. You will need a 'light bank' to give them 24-hour light.

- To promote interest during this topic, grow your own tomatoes as an ongoing activity. They will grow on a windowsill in a growbag. Plant them out when they are about 10 cm tall.

- Sunflower seeds are large and the plants grow quickly and tall. These could be grown and then taken home by the students. Starting these off to germinate at the start of this topic would provide plants to work with later.

- Many beans grow during most times of the year, if kept in a warm place. Allowing students to plant seeds and watch them grow, especially if they can eat the produce, is a great way of ensuring they try to look after their plants well.

Knowledge check

- Younger students have difficulty understanding growth. Some may still think that they grow once a year, on their birthday. They may imagine that plants grow because they swell – rather like a balloon. Individual plant cells fill with water and swell to produce the rapid elongation of shoots and roots. But most growth is by cell division – the splitting of cells to increase the number, not the volume of cells. The subsequent swelling of the new cells leads to permanent growth. Some of these new cells, of course, will become specialized structures – flowers, fruits and new leaves.

- Many students are unaware that plants grow from seeds. Others may believe that seeds only arrive in packets. Some are unaware that grass and trees are both green plants. They may only recognize a green plant when it is a flower. Many do not understand that trees are living things.

Skills check

Students need to:

- identify differences between animals and plants

- make careful observations and measurements

- collect evidence and decide how good it is

- use their evidence to explain what they found out.

Some students will:

- suggest why growing a number of plants provides better evidence than growing one.

Links to other subjects

Literacy: Reading and following simple instructions, e.g. setting up the stem activity. Comparing a variety of information texts including IT-based sources. Reading information passages and identifying main points of text.

Numeracy: Measuring and comparing using standard units. Organizing and interpreting simple data in bar graphs or line graphs.

ICT: Using a digital camera. Using a multimedia package to combine text and graphics to make a presentation.

Art: Exploring line, shape, colour and texture in natural forms, e.g. leaf skeletons.

Let's find out...

The Unit opens with this question:

> Gardeners mainly buy plants at the start of the growing season. Shops make sure that there are young plants for people to buy, but how can they control the way the plants grow, so that they are not too big or too small?

Discuss the problem. Encourage students to make suggestions or predictions. Note any misconceptions and probe to find the reasons why they believe what they say. Tell them that they are going to learn about how plants grow so that they can solve the problem.

41

Unit 2: Helping plants grow well – Sorting plants into groups

The objectives for this lesson are that students should be able to:

- Explain how plants are living things even if they don't move

- Learn how to group plants using their similarities and differences

- Discover how to use a branching key to sort plants

- Make a branching key of their own.

SB pp.24–25

Starter

- Bring in a set of manageable objects such as toys, vegetables, cups and plates, that can be sorted in a variety of ways. Put them in two groups, perhaps with two hoops, while the students watch. Perhaps they will offer suggestions. Then ask them, 'What's my rule?' (Red and not red, for example.) Encourage students always to be able to explain the reasons for their choices. Take all the objects out and use another secret rule. Show how the objects can be sorted according to your rule.

- Ask students to do the same with a set of objects. What's their rule? (Careful – it might be 'I just like all these'.) Ask them to sort by different rules.

Explain

Living and non-living

Students may find it hard to believe that plants are living because they don't 'do' anything. But plants are, of course, growing and changing, and they reproduce (spectacularly in some cases, with flowers).

Different plants

By answering a series of questions, you narrow down your unknown rule until it is firmly identified. Branching keys for all the wild flowers you are likely to find tend to run over several pages, and get into complex structural questions, but a small key of the plants in your school garden is easier to use. It's also a good exercise for students, whether in using one or in constructing one.

The idea is to ask questions that split the unknowns into smaller and smaller groups. Take an orange, an apple and a banana. Several questions are possible, but the first might be 'Is it round?' The orange and the apple are, but the banana is not. The first question can, sometimes, identify something. Now we have two more items to classify, and the next question might be 'Is it green?' That divides the two and identifies each.

Some plants have flowers

Plant classification is complex and based on issues such as whether the seeds have a single seed leaf, (like grasses, bamboos and palms) or two (like most other green plants). At this level, it is most important to present the idea of similarities and differences – and that simple yes/no questions can help sort and name them.

Things to do

Sorting into groups

Help students group objects by, for example, using vegetables. Ask students to describe a vegetable they are holding. Ask them to guess which vegetables you are describing from the group on your table. Ask them to describe one vegetable on the table and for the rest of the class to guess which one it is. Finally, ask them to guess which vegetable you have behind your back by asking you questions you can answer with 'yes' or 'no'. Point out that each step in the description makes identification easier – the more you know, the more easily you reject some.

Make a branching key

Split four plants into two groups. Challenge the students to explain your criteria. For example, you might group all long-leaf plants on one side, all broad-leaf plants on the other; all those with flowers on one side, all those without on the other; all having fruits with one seed on one side, many-seeded fruits on the other; and so on. Ask 'What is the single question that separates the two groups?'

Show how the questions you ask can result in different divisions. Now ask for another question, subdividing one of the two big groups. Perhaps an

42

individual plant can now be identified since it falls into a 'group of one'. Ask the students to think of questions that will do this. The students can make a branching key to record.

Record

Completed branching keys are themselves a good record for learning. Large-scale copies could be displayed, together with the sorted plants.

Support

Draw branching keys on large sheets of paper and ask students to move real objects down the 'tracks' of the key to separate them, either by answering questions set by you or making up questions themselves.

Extend

Students could use sticky labels to cover parts of a branching key and test each other: 'What goes here?' or 'What question did I ask here?'

Dig deeper

Students have the opportunity to find out more about different types of plants.

I wonder...

Until quite recently, mushrooms and other fungi were grouped with the plants. But there are distinct differences. They are saprophytes – they do not manufacture their own food as flowering plants do. Their cell walls are not made of cellulose. Fungi are now grouped as a separate kingdom.

Other ideas

Using a branching key

Show how the careful choice of questions makes a branching key work well. It's easy to find a question that isolates one object, but that still leaves you with a big group to sort. You need early questions that will result in two big, but distinctive, groups. Depending on the questions, some groups may be empty. You should not end up with two objects in one group!

ICT ideas

Keys for plants make it easy to name them and keys like this are ideal for ICT use. Many computer programs make use of a similar branching key. Screens ask you the questions and, according to your response, lead you down a particular path.

At home
WS 13

Ask students to complete WS 13. Then they can devise a branching key that will sort their family or friends.

Plenary

You might look at some common examples of plant keys in identification books.

New International Edition

Unit 2: Helping plants grow well – Growing plants

The objectives for this lesson are that students should be able to:

- Discover how fast plants can grow

- Plan and take part in a scientific investigation

- Present and communicate findings

- Understand that a plant needs leaves to grow well.

SB pp.26–27   *Starter*

Note: Activities in this Unit will take a month or more and should be set up as early as possible in the topic.

- Show the students a pot plant. Explain that it was once smaller, but it got too big for its pot. *I bought it a month ago and it was nice and small. Now look at it! It's bursting out of its pot. How has this happened? I haven't been feeding it. In fact, I gave it scrambled egg yesterday and it didn't eat any of it! What's going on? How can it grow without food? How do you think you could find out?*

The challenge

Read the speech bubbles on page 26 in the *Student Book*. Discuss the different ways the groups in Class 3 decided to record growth. *Why were these good or not so good ideas?* Give each group of students a small pot plant to look after for a month to see how much it grows. Ask them to think about what they will do.

What to do

If you want a table or graph from this activity, encourage the students to measure regularly. Let them record their measurements on a table – perhaps kept close to the plant – noting date of measurement and plant height.

What you need

- small pot plants with different numbers of leaves

- measuring sticks or tapes

- simple watering systems, e.g. use small containers to measure watering

- digital camera or a video camera with a timer

- a balance or scales

What to check

This is a fair test only if conditions such as the initial size of the plants and where the plants are placed to grow are controlled. Make sure the students understand how important it is to take measurements from the same point or photographs from the same position and in a similar light. When pictures are imported into multimedia presentation software, setting slides to change automatically will give the effect of the plant growing. Ensure students measure from the same datum line all the time – this will probably be the surface of the soil.

Support

Discuss how the plants should be treated to make the results valid. Point out that treating plants differently will give different results. So will measuring different things. Agree on a 'fair' measurement.

Extend

Expect all students to be able to point to the tallest and shortest plants; expect most to make cause and effect connections, e.g. we had the most leaves on our plant, which is why it grew well. Let some students weigh and measure their plants every day to give an accurate picture and produce a critical approach as to the validity of their results when measuring or weighing.

Some students might notice the way plants grow – the bigger the plant, the more plant material they add so they weigh more.

What did you find?   WS 14   WS 15

The students should use the table provided on WS 14. They should record the number of leaves each plant has at the start of the experiment and then record their results every day.

Record

Encourage the students to convert their recorded data into a graph. As a fallback, they could use Class 3's data given in the *Student Book* and on WS 15. The data is continuous – plants grow steadily – so it should be represented as a line graph. Line graphs are more appropriate to older students who already have a clear understanding of what a bar chart represents. You may choose to draw a line graph anyway, or you may work on their understanding of bar charts by drawing the results as a stick graph. Stick graphs bridge the bar chart/line graph gap. If appropriate, use the spreadsheet software to convert the table into a chart or graph.

Present

Ask the students to look at the chart or graph and 'tell its story'. *Once the plant was tiny, then…* Encourage them to write what they did and what they saw, including drawing the table of results and chart.

Let each group of students present their findings to another class. If they have taken photographs or video clips, encourage them to import these to show how the plant grew. They should also include their table of results and charts or graphs.

Can you do better?

Ask students to review how good their evidence was. How would they tackle the investigation differently if they were starting again?

Show the students Class 3's report on WS 15 and read it together. Do they notice that the results table shows a plant with three leaves, although there is no mention of this earlier in the report?

What do they think about this? Has Class 3 drawn the right conclusions from the results? What could they have done better? Ask the students to criticize the report.

Now predict

Discuss the results and check that the students understand that the plant needs leaves to grow well. A plant will grow better and faster if it has plenty of leaves, so the advice should be to make sure the plant has lots of green leaves before you buy it.

Other ideas

Plant races

Compare the growth of two different types of plant. Do different types of plant grow at different rates? Compare the growth of all the groups' plants. Consider awarding a prize for the plant that has grown the most.

Data logging

Use data logging to measure and record the conditions – light, temperature – that your plants experience.

If you connect a digital balance to your computer, you can use data logging to measure the mass of the plant as it changes over the month.

At home

WS 16

Students could take seeds, planted seeds or potted seedlings to grow at home. Arrange a day to bring them back to school. Compare their growth and growing conditions.

Ask students to complete WS 16 as homework.

Plenary

It is essential that students explain their discoveries. Observations are not enough. They should be linking them to their understanding, e.g. 'Our plant grew well because it had more leaves.' Remind the students of the predictions they made before starting the investigation. Were they right? Did they guess correctly that a plant needs its leaves to grow well?

New International Edition

Unit 2: Helping plants grow well – Roots and stems

The objectives for this lesson are that students should be able to:

- Learn that plants need roots to stay upright

- Discover how plants get water and nutrients through their roots

- Make predictions on what will happen in the investigation

- Draw diagrams showing how plants take up coloured water.

SB pp.28–29 — Starter

- Show a picture of different-sized pot plants. *Why is the bigger plant in the bigger pot? Is the pot big because the plant is big? Or is the plant big because the pot is big?*

- Show the students a pot plant that is pot-bound, with the roots coming out of the bottom of the pot. Repot it in front of the students to show that the roots would like more space. Liken this to having shoes that are too tight. *What do you do about it? How do you feel with a larger pair?*

- Wear a jumper or shirt that is too small and ask the students why you feel so uncomfortable. *What can I do about it?* The students should suggest that you need to buy bigger clothes. Link this to plants needing space for their roots.

Explain

Plants need roots

Discuss how plants need roots to take in water from the soil. Without healthy roots, plants can't grow. Look at the bean seeds planted in the first lesson. These should illustrate that the water is taken in through the roots. Roots are in contact with the water as can be seen through the sides of the jam jar.

The water goes up

Explain that plants take in water through their roots. Some students may think that they 'drink' rainwater through their leaves. Some water is taken in this way but most is drawn up through the roots. When watering plants, it is most effective to pour water at the base of the stem, not over the whole plant from above. This is how most irrigation systems work. Ask the students to imagine how much mopping up would be needed if indoor plants were watered from above!

Things to do

Coloured celery

Examine cut stems from different plants and look for the tubes that carry the water through the plant. The water rises up the stem. Colour the water with ink or food colouring and in time you will see the colour in the tubes if you carefully cut across the stem. Use table knives for the splitting and cutting to reduce the risk of injury, or do all the cutting yourself with a scalpel blade (this will make a cleaner cut and avoid damaging the tubes). The pigment will gradually colour the whole stem. Using a hairdryer on the leaves will speed up the process or use slightly wilted specimens, which draw up water faster. The tubes are like straws, with the water being sucked up by the leaves.

Record

Annotated drawings will make clear both what the students did and what they observed. Ask them to colour their diagrams and explain what they saw.

Support

Ask the students what they think they will see if they cut the celery higher up and lower down. They may find that the upper part of the celery is still white. Can they explain why?

Extend

Split the base of the stem and put half in one colour and half in another. Because the tubes in the stem are vertical, each half will be coloured differently. White carnations colour well too. Keeping carnations out of water for some time before you use them speeds up the outcome.

Ask students what would happen if you mixed two different inks in the same glass and put the flower in. The flower would turn a mixture of the ink colours, rather than some parts being one colour and some the other.

Dig deeper

Students have the opportunity to find out what plants use water for: cooling, transport and photosynthesis.

Did you know?

These facts remind students that water is taken in through the roots and is needed for growth.

- In the hot summer, some plants stay green when the surrounding grass is brown. Their roots are so long that they can find water far under dry ground. They don't dry out like the grass plants. Try digging up one of these plants to see its roots – every piece left behind can grow to make a new plant!

I wonder...

Students will see the veins in the leaf. These vary in pattern. Leaf rubbings will record the different vein patterns. You can find leaf skeletons in the autumn when the leaf material has decayed.

Other ideas

Automatic watering

Set a design and technology task to plan a simple watering device for a school plant. Students' designs may include using a fine tube or a strip of ribbon to take the water from a reservoir, or leaving a huge block of ice to melt slowly over the holiday.

Plant straws

As well as cutting the stem of the celery crossways to see the tubes, try cutting the stem lengthways and trying to follow the tubes as they go up the stem. If you leave them until they are all inky, it is easier to see. These tubes are called 'xylem'. They run alongside another set of tubes called 'phloem', through which the sugar and starch produced by the leaves are carried to the rest of the plant.

Presentation

Let the students imagine they are botanists and ask them to work in groups to prepare a PowerPoint presentation explaining why a plant contains tubes. They should include information on how to produce coloured flowers.

Although short-lived, a display of all the different colours of flowers or celery you have produced is attractive. The colour does intensify over time.

At home

WS 17

Ask the students to create a black flower. They can use any flower they like, but the best ones are white with straight, strong stems to stand in water and ink. They can also complete WS 17 to consolidate their learning.

Plenary

Produce a flower with four colours, i.e. split the stem into four and place each part into a different colour of ink. Ask the students how you did it. Ask how you could do it more quickly, i.e. use a wilted plant or put it on a sunny windowsill. Ask the students how to make the colour deeper in the leaves/flower and then how to make it fade again. The colour will not be lost completely, though.

New International Edition

Unit 2: Helping plants grow well – Plants and water

The objectives for this lesson are that students should be able to:

- Find out how much water plants and growing seeds need

- Investigate the best conditions for plants to grow well

- Present and communicate their results

- Learn why they should base their findings on more than one example.

SB pp.30–31   *Starter*

Note: It will take about 10 to 14 days for the seeds to germinate.

- Use a picture of trees to show that plants can be grown in wet ground, then show a picture of a cactus. *These two plants have changed so that they can cope with different amounts of water. But we can make sure our houseplants have just the right amount – not too little, not too much.*

- Show the students two sick-looking plants: one swimming in water and one in bone-dry soil. If plants aren't available, then use seeds: have one seed swimming in water and one on dry cotton wool. Discuss which will survive and germinate best.

The challenge

Read What to do and the speech bubbles on page 30 in the *Student Book*. Discuss the different ways the groups in Class 3 decided to set up their experiment. Why were these good or not so good ideas? Give each group a packet of seeds and ask them to decide how they will work out how much water a seed needs to grow. What do they think will happen with each set-up they design?

What to do

The challenge is to germinate the seeds and provide them with enough water to grow well. The best way to establish that the evidence is reliable is to use more than one seed. The students will need to measure carefully the amount of water they give the seeds. They will also need to decide where to place them.

What you need

- small, rapid-germinating seeds

- saucers and cotton wool

- measuring sticks or tapes

- measuring cylinders or jugs

- a digital camera or a video camera with a timer

What to check

This is a fair test only if conditions, such as where the plant is placed to grow, are controlled. Discuss this to make sure the students understand how important it is to take measurements from the same point, or photographs from the same position and in a similar light. Students should measure the same quantity each time, either the number of seeds that have germinated, or how tall the plants have become.

Support

Students might need help identifying a germinating seed in its early stages. This is when the root first comes out of the seed coat.

Extend

Expect all students to be able to indicate which dish of seeds produced the most germinated seeds. Some students may start to measure the growth of the seedlings and from this understand that the seedlings need a small amount of water to grow well, but not too much. Let them give each dish a set amount of water each day and measure the growth of the seedlings.

What did you find?   WS 18

The students should use the table provided on WS 18 to record the number of seeds that have germinated. They can also use WS 18 to summarize their evidence.

Record

They should convert their data into a graph. As a fallback, they could use Class 3's data given in the *Student Book*. The data is continuous as plants grow steadily and should be represented correctly as a line graph.

Present

Ask students to use the graph to say which amount of water was best for starting plant growth, and then present their findings in groups. Any photographs or video clips taken can be imported to show how the plant grew. They should also include their table of results and charts or graphs.

Can you do better?

WS 19

What did you find difficult in this experiment? If the seeds were small, they might have been difficult to see, making germination difficult to observe.

Read together Class 3's report on WS 19. *Do you think Class 3 has drawn the right conclusions from their results?* Ask the students to criticize the report. How do their reports compare with Class 3's?

Students find it easy to spot the winners and losers. Encourage them to recognize more general statements, e.g. some watering is essential for seeds to germinate at all.

Now predict

The amount of water given to the seed will depend on how dry or wet it is before you water it. It will need watering after germination so that it can continue to grow.

Using ten seeds per dish instead of one provides more consistent information. For example, the one seed planted might be dead or rotten to start with, or it might have started to germinate from the conditions it was kept in previously.

Other ideas

Watering plants

Let students do a similar experiment with the bean seedlings they planted at the beginning of the topic, checking the height of the plant rather than how many seeds germinated.

Soil-less plants

Find out if plants really need soil as well as water. Push three cocktail sticks into a potato or avocado seed at about the same level all the way round. Place the potato in a glass or cup with about one-third of the potato in water and the sticks resting on the side of the glass. Place it in a sunny spot and see if roots grow. Leave for even longer to see if it produces leaves as well. Plants also need the mineral salts from soil, of course.

At home

Students can explore how plants in the garden get their water and what happens to them if they don't get water. From here, talk about plants thriving in conditions that suit them, e.g. in a dry garden the plants that do well are those that need little water.

Plenary

It is essential that students link their discoveries to their understanding, e.g. 'Our plant grew well because it had just the right amount of water' or 'Our seeds germinated because they had just the right amount of water'. Remind them of the predictions they made before starting. Were they right? Did they guess correctly that a seed needs water to germinate? Did they predict the amount?

Unit 2: Helping plants grow well – Plants and light

The objectives for this lesson are that students should be able to:

- Understand that plants need light as well as water to grow well

- Find out why leaves are green

- Learn how plants use their leaves and light to make food

- Plan and present a report using ICT.

SB pp.32–33

Starter

- Display a photo of a wilting plant. *What is wrong with this plant? Where do you think it has been growing?*

- Show the students two pots of grass or two pot plants, one kept in the dark and one in the light (or take them outside to some grass covered earlier in plastic). *Why is one yellow and one green? What has one plant not had?*

- Show some celery with the tops on. *How are the stems grown to be so white?* They are forced through more and more soil, so that the stems don't have access to the light. Rhubarb is grown in a similar way, but the stems are coloured with pigments that are not affected by light.

Explain

Reach for it!

Sunflowers grow quickly in warmth and sunlight. Their flowers grow towards the Sun. Like most plants, they follow the Sun across the sky during the day. All plants have 'sleep' patterns. When the Sun goes down at night, the leaves and flowers will droop. They will perk up again as soon as the Sun rises.

Tall trees, spreading leaves

Competition for light is the cause of both of these. Plants that grow tall or climb up other plants or buildings will reach and exploit the sunlight, especially in crowded conditions like a forest. When a tall tree falls, many small trees take its place.

Things to do

Why are leaves green?

The area hidden by the foil on the leaf has not had any sunlight. This means that the green colouring, chlorophyll, is not being used, so the leaf turns pale green or yellow. It is best to do this activity either with plenty of sunlight or with a lamp facing the plants. This will promote the use of the chlorophyll, so the students will notice the loss faster in the covered patch. Leave the lamp on overnight if you can.

Record

Students can stick their foil shape and leaf into their books or on paper and label where the sunlight has been.

Support

Discuss why you don't let the students check under the foil every day – it lets light in!

Extend

All students should be able to recognize that without sunlight, a plant's leaves go paler or yellow. Some students may like to look at a variegated leaf and then predict which part of the leaf makes the food. If you keep a variegated plant in shady conditions, it loses its variegation. It produces more chlorophyll to photosynthesize in lower light levels, and goes yellow.

Exploring

Leaves are green because they contain chloroplasts, which contain chlorophyll. This chemical enables the plant to use the Sun's energy to convert carbon dioxide and water to sugars and oxygen. It only absorbs certain wavelengths of light and reflects the green. Therefore it appears green.

Did you know?

These facts remind students that plants can grow very big and that they grow towards the light.

- The giant Victoria water lily from South America may grow leaves strong enough to support a small child.

I wonder...

Seeds commonly germinate without light, of course. Plants can grow without light, using food stores from the seed, but their desperate need for light is illustrated by their long and straggling growth in search of it. Without light, they will eventually die.

Other ideas

Turning to the Sun

Seedlings grown on a windowsill will turn their leaves to face the light. Turning the seedlings round shows how, in time, they change to face the light again. A simple plastic mirror or sheet of cooking foil put behind the seedlings reflects the light and they will grow straight upwards in these balanced light conditions.

Time lapse

If you have access to time lapse on a digital camera or on a video camera, watching a plant for a single day, taking a picture every 5 minutes, then running at normal speed, will show the plant's leaves or flowers following the Sun across the sky. Continuing at night, with a low level of light, will allow the film to then show how the plant has a 'sleep' pattern.

Presentation

Ask students to write a report using word-processing software to explain how a plant turns its leaves around to face the light.

At home

WS 20

Ask the students to observe some plants outside, either on the way home or in the garden, to see which way their leaves generally face. Can they explain why some plants' leaves don't face any particular direction? This is due to the Sun appearing to move across the sky. When plants have grown too big to follow the Sun, they gain a maximum amount of light by having leaves facing in all directions. Ask the students to explain to a family member why the leaves follow the Sun around during the day.

Ask the students to complete WS 20 to consolidate their learning.

Plenary

Show the students a dish of yellow seedlings, or a different plant that has been kept in the dark, and ask them to describe what has happened. Ask them how they can make the plant green again.

New International Edition

Unit 2: Helping plants grow well – Plants and warmth

The objectives for this lesson are that students should be able to:

- Learn that plants grow best when they have warmth, light, air and water

- Find out about why plants grow well in glasshouses

- Plan and take part in a scientific experiment

- Understand that water evaporates from leaves.

SB pp.34–35   Starter

- Show the students a picture of a rainforest. *Why are these plants so big? Where do you think they are growing?* Discuss the weather conditions in tropical countries.

- Show the students two different-sized plants or vegetables. Imply that being kept warm has made one grow faster.

- Set up a thermometer in the window and also one outside. Let the students look at them and see that the thermometer inside has a different reading from the one outside. Some students might need help reading the thermometers.

- If you have access to a sunny room with lots of windows and no air conditioning, spend some time in there to prove that it is warmer under glass. A visit to a glasshouse or garden centre is even better.

Explain

Warmer and warmer

A glasshouse traps sunlight by allowing the warmth in. The glass reflects the trapped warmth back into the glasshouse. This means the air in the glasshouse keeps getting warmer.

Where does the water go?

When we sweat, it is called 'perspiration'. Plants have a similar process called 'transpiration'. The water is lost from the underside of the leaves through small holes called 'stomata'.

Cacti don't want to lose water as they would quickly dry out. They do not have large, flat leaves; the smaller the leaf, the less surface and the less water loss. Cacti also have fleshy stems

that store water whenever it rains. Plants that live in the jungle, where it is very humid, have very large leaves to allow them to lose water easily. Some plants have very fleshy leaves in which they store water.

Things to do

Quick growers

Challenging the students to use all the information they have been given so far to produce the first seedlings and the tallest plants is a fun and ongoing project.

> ⚠ If you plan to eat your plant products, don't forget to obtain parental permission.

Record

A picture of the plants and seedlings they grew with a list of bullet points to say where they grew them and why those places were best can be referred to later. They will provide a summary of the topic.

Support

Remind students of how much water they needed to give to their seeds in the watering experiments, so that they can plan how much to give their seedlings.

Extend

Most students should recognize that their seeds need water, warmth and light. Some might realize that seeds don't actually need light to germinate, just to grow healthily afterwards, as they often germinate underground. The fridge is not a fair place to grow plants, since it removes both light and heat at the same time.

Dig deeper

Students have the opportunity to find out how plants survive in the desert, where water is rare.

Did you know?

These facts remind students that plants require water to remain healthy. They also remind students that we use plants for a variety of purposes.

52

I wonder...

Without the Sun, there would be no light for the plants to photosynthesize. There would be no warmth for them to grow well either. Without photosynthesis, they will not produce oxygen for us to breathe or food for us to eat, so all animals not already killed by the cold, dark conditions would eventually die.

Other ideas

Sweaty plants

Place a plastic bag over a plant and tie it around the stem. Pull the bag out above the tie to create a reservoir to collect liquid. Place the plant in a sunny spot so that it starts to lose water. You should see water condensing and then running down the sides of the bag. This will prove that water is lost from the leaves. If students ask about losing water from the roots and soil, cover the surface of the soil with cling film.

Most wilted

Speed up transpiration by creating a flow of air across a plant. This makes water evaporation take place faster, just as it does when we sweat. The more air that passes over, the more the plant wilts. Set a design and technology task for the students to produce an automatic fan system to make a plant wilt more.

Presentation

In groups, let the students pretend that they are giving a demonstration in a garden centre. Using a large poster or diagram, they need to explain why a plant must be watered regularly. They should talk about water being taken in through the roots and then travelling up through the tubes and being lost through the leaves. The pores in the leaves are called stomata.

At home

WS 21

Ask the students to observe some plants both at home, outside and in school. Can they guess what sort of climate the plants came from by looking at and feeling the leaves? They should record their predictions on WS 21. They should find out that many indoor plants come from a tropical area, since they are used to more heat and humidity.

Plenary

Discuss where the water comes from that the plants lose through their leaves. Ask the students in what sort of weather plants will lose most water. The lost water is drawn up by the leaves from the roots and so from the soil. Some of this water is used to produce oxygen and carbohydrates through photosynthesis. Some is retained by the plant to fill cells; some is lost by transpiration – cooling the leaves.

Unit 2: Helping plants grow well – Plants and seeds

The objectives for this lesson are that students should be able to:

- Learn how plants reproduce by making seeds that grow into new plants
- Find out about how plants are pollinated
- Understand that seed sizes vary greatly and are unique to their plant
- Make a record of what seeds they eat at home.

Starter
SB pp.36–37

- Bring in two kinds of flower. Make one a spectacular coloured flower and the other one the insignificant flower of a grass or other cereal, or of a tree. Compare the two and explain to students that while the coloured flower attracts insects, the other flower is pollinated by the wind.

- Prepare a collection of seeds in advance. A very few seeds (some beans for example) may be poisonous when raw so select them with care. Aim for variety, from a large avocado nut to tiny powdery seeds. Discuss with the students how important the seeds are to green plants.

Explain

Flowers

Pictures and examples of the flowers of different plants will help students to understand that not all flowers are easily recognized. Students could sort them into insect-pollinated and wind-pollinated. You can teach them more about the structure of flowers.

Bees and pollen

Teach students about the importance of insects in the pollination of many plants. If possible, show examples of pollen, which when magnified have strikingly different colours and coats. Ask them to find out more about the honeybee and the way in which it acts as a pollinator.

Things to do

Different seeds

Some students may believe that seeds come from packets. Challenge this by presenting seeds found in their local habitat, including some that are still in their seed cases.

Grow a number of different seeds, proving that each seed is unique to the type of plant.

Record

Record the sizes and shapes of different seeds and begin to think about the ways in which these different seeds are dispersed.

Support

Many students have a very narrow concept of what constitutes a plant. Many will not believe that a tree and even grass are examples of plants. Give them every opportunity to experience different kinds of plants and to recognize that these are living things.

Extend

Play a game in an open area where the majority of the students form small circles. Each circle is a flower head. Give each flower a drink in a cup and give each student a drinking straw. Give the students in each flower a soft foam ball. A handful of the students are pollinating bees. They go to a flower, drink from the cup using their straws, and are given some foam-ball pollen to carry. They go to another flower, drink again, and leave the pollen behind. The game is enhanced if the students playing the bees wear striped T-shirts and if the pollen balls are covered in Velcro. Then they will stick to the bees' clothing.

Dig deeper

Students have the opportunity to find out more about flowering plants and how they reproduce.

Did you know?

- Students are always interested in extremes and the coconut and the avocado nut are interesting as extreme examples of seed size. The largest seed in the world is that of the coco de mer, which can weigh up to 20 kg and can be larger than a basketball.

- Students will be surprised to find how many seeds they routinely eat as part of their diet. These include peas, beans and other pulses.

I wonder...

Many flowers will self-pollinate if not cross-pollinated from another flower. In some cases, the male anther bends to touch the stigma of the same flower.

Other ideas

Pollination

Explore pollination in the classroom by getting students to use a soft paintbrush to transfer pollen from one flower to another. They are acting as the pollinator. Does this increase the yield of fruits and seeds from the pollinated plants?

Presentation

Other classes might enjoy watching the pollination game played by your students. With a little effort, students could make themselves look like the petals of a flower or a bee with antennae and even wings.

At home

Ask students to record when they eat seeds as part of a meal. Remind them that this includes bread and other wheat products, maize products and a great many vegetables.

Plenary

Seeds disperse plants and make it possible for them to invade new areas. Look around safe areas of the school grounds for examples of plant invasion. If you have an area that has recently been dug over, you may see the first plants taking advantage of the broken ground. Many weeds are opportunists, growing quickly and vigorously from seeds landing in broken ground.

55

Unit 2: Helping plants grow well – Unit 2: Review

The objectives for this lesson are that students should be able to:

- Check what they have learned in this Unit about helping plants grow well

- Find out how they are working towards, within and beyond the Grade 3 level.

SB p.38

Expectations

Students working towards Grade 3 level will:

- Recognize that living things grow and reproduce, and that plants are living things

- Recognize that plants need light, warmth and water to grow

- Put plants into groups

- Make some measurements of the height of plants.

In addition, students working within Grade 3 level will:

- Recognize that plants provide food for humans and other animals

- Recognize that a branching key helps put things into groups by asking questions

- Name the parts of a plant that are needed for it to grow well

- Recognize that plant growth is affected by temperature, amount of water and light

- Make careful measurements of volumes of water and height of plants

- Recognize that in experiments and investigations, a number of plants need to be used to provide reliable evidence

- Draw simple conclusions from their investigations.

Further to this, students working beyond Grade 3 level will also:

- Explain why healthy roots and a healthy stem are needed for plants to grow

- Recognize that the leaves of a plant are associated with healthy growth

- Begin to use a branching key to identify plants

- Explain in simple terms why a number of plants should be used to provide reliable evidence about plant growth

- Present their results in a variety of ways.

Check-up

Discuss the two different situations with the students. They should be able to tell you that the plants in Class 3S would grow better because:

- they had constant water, which is a raw material for growing plant material

- they had constant light, which is essential to healthy plant growth

- they had warmth, which accelerates the growth of plants.

Check that the students have written the correct instructions for growing seeds. They could use a drawing program to design a seed packet and import their text instructions.

Assessment

WS 22

Use the Unit 2 assessment on WS 22 to check the students' understanding of the content of the Unit. The answers are given opposite.

Name: _____ Date: _____

WS 22 Unit 2 assessment

1 Class 3 grew some plants in the same way from the same packet of seeds. They started them all together.

Condition	Plant height after 10 days (cm)
Watered in a cold room	3
No water in a cold room	0
Watered on a warm windowsill	7
No water on a warm windowsill	0

a) What conditions were best? _____
b) Why did the plants grow best in these conditions.
_____
c) Why was this a fair test. _____

2 Raj's grandad grew a carrot top. Raj put some carrot tops in a saucer of water on the windowsill. He put water in the saucer when it was dry. After several days, the carrot tops grew green leaves. They were like tiny palm trees. Then Raj forgot to water them and the leaves wilted.
3 a) Why did Raj's grandad put the carrot tops on the windowsill?
_____
b) Why did he water them? _____
c) How could the carrot tops grow without food?
_____
d) Why did the leaves wilt when Raj forgot to water them?

22   Heinemann Explore Science Grade 3

Answers

1   **a**   Watered in light, warm conditions.

    b   Seeds will not germinate ('start') without water. Heat and light accelerate growth. Water is a raw material of plant growth.

    c   The same seeds from the same packet were used. All that differed were the growing conditions.

2   **a**   Light and warmth speed up growth.

    b   Water is a raw material for growing plant material.

    c   The leaves of the carrot tops used light energy, water (and carbon dioxide) to make more plant material.

    d   Without water, the carrot could no longer stay alive. The leaves lost their stiffness and health.

The answer!

Refer back to the introductory question. Discuss the fact that shops and garden centres control the heat and light in glasshouses to ensure plants are ready at the time they are in demand. Try to organize a gardener or horticulturalist to visit and explain or show how plants are 'brought on' by heat and other conditions.

And finally...

Set up a 'garden centre' for other classes to see. Show a range of plants, e.g. grass and a Bonsai tree, with the question, 'Is this a plant?' Show a range of plant products, including plant foods. Show the enquiry results, graphs and conclusions. If equipment is available, set up some of the students' PowerPoint presentations to run automatically on a computer screen near the display.

New International Edition

Unit 3: Characteristics of materials

The objectives for this Unit are that students should be able to:

- Learn more about the materials around them
- Discover that a quality of a material is called a property
- Find out how different materials are better for different tasks
- Make predictions and collect evidence to check predictions.

SB p.39 *Science background*

The word 'material' is often used to describe cloth or fabric. However, in science it describes all the 'stuff' in the world, and the word 'fabric' should be used for cloth alone.

Learning more about the materials around them is a basis for students' future understanding of chemistry. Through primary science experiences, students encounter, explore, change and use a wide range of everyday materials.

The dividing line between something that is entirely natural, such as a piece of wood, and entirely synthetic or artificial, such as plastic, is hard to define in simple terms. Although plastic is made from oil, a natural resource, it is not a natural material. Even so-called natural materials are usually shaped to make them useful. Wool, for instance, is a natural material that can be dyed or woven. Perhaps a truly natural garment is something like an untreated animal skin that is worn as it is. Encourage students to make their own definitions, e.g. if it still looks like the original natural material, it is classed as natural.

Language

Absorbent	Has the ability to 'soak up' liquid.
Brittle	Splinters or shatters easily.
Natural	Obtained from a natural source, e.g. wood, stone.
Transparent	Allows most light to pass through.
Translucent	Allows some light through.
Opaque	Allows very little or no light through.

The Words to learn list on page 39 of the *Student Book* can be used to make a classroom display.

Resources

- *Properties of Materials* Reader.
- Common objects made of different materials, e.g. spoons, knives, plates.
- A range of objects made from the same material, e.g. metals, plastics.
- A range of plastic bags, paper bags and leather bags.
- Masses.
- Measuring tools.
- A selection of socks in different thicknesses, colours and sizes.
- Different types of paper, e.g. paper towel, copy paper, filter paper, blotting paper, sugar paper, backing/display paper.
- Ink.
- Small beakers or glasses.
- A digital microscope (optional).
- A video camera.
- A light sensor.
- Samples of materials, including metals and wood.
- Chocolate.
- A digital camera.
- Stopwatches.
- Food colouring.

Bright ideas

- Use a digital camera to take shots of materials around the school or during the enquiries so that they can be used in presentations.
- Use a video camera during enquiries and then run at fast speed to show the effect of the experiment.
- After the bridges experiment, the materials could be examined under a digital microscope. They should show some signs of stress, including cracks.
- Use a light sensor for the Not as tough as boots activity in the Comparing materials lesson. This relates to the challenge in the Clean teeth lesson of Unit 1: Living and growing.

Knowledge check

- All students will know a range of materials from fabric to wood, plastic and metal. Some may be able to recognize metals such as gold, silver and iron. Metals may all be classed as 'iron' unless they are a different colour, like gold or copper.

- Students should be aware that every material has several properties, e.g. most plastic is bendy and smooth, and most metal is strong and shiny. A good starter would be to brainstorm all the words the students use to identify materials, e.g. shiny, colour, texture, bendy/flexible. Explain that science words to describe properties of materials generally come in pairs of opposites, e.g. rough, smooth, hard, soft and so on.

Skills check

Students need to:

- measure length
- make observations and comparisons
- use appropriate vocabulary.

Some students will:

- name some specific metals
- represent measurements in a bar chart
- explain how to structure a fair test.

Links to other subjects

Literacy: Writing instructions. Making clear notes. Writing definitions of words.

Numeracy: Measuring mass and length. Organizing and interpreting simple data in bar graphs or line graphs.

ICT: Using a digital camera, video or digital microscope. Using a multimedia package to combine text and graphics to make a presentation.

Design and technology: Making bridges from paper straws. Designing and making an object from a material, based on the properties that are suited to the object.

History: Learning how plastic was discovered.

Let's find out...

The Unit opens with this question:

Tyres are made of rubber. Some shoe soles are made of rubber. Why is rubber the best choice of material for these things? The soles of our shoes are not as thick as tyres. Why does the tyre need to be thicker?

Discuss the question. As the topic progresses, students will have the opportunity to experiment with materials and discover their properties. They will also experience the effect of wear on the materials, so should be able to suggest why rubber is used and why it has to be different thicknesses.

New International Edition

Unit 3: Characteristics of materials – Different materials

The objectives for this lesson are that students should be able to:

- Find out that all kinds of 'stuff' make materials

- Record materials around their school and explain how they recognized them

- Discover that the same material can do different jobs

- Understand that some materials are natural and some are man-made.

SB pp.40–41 — Starter

- Present a wide variety of safe materials and objects and ask the students to group them according to their own rules. Include clothes, books and kitchen utensils, as well as pieces of cloth, wool and blocks of raw materials, such as metals and wood. When the items have been grouped, invite the students to guess what the different groups' rules were. For instance, they could be grouped under 'bendy' and 'stiff', or 'metal' and 'not metal'. Repeat the activity, this time grouping the items using different rules.

- Talk about the many ways of classifying materials. They can be divided into solids, liquids and gases. Some can be put into more than one group; some, such as water, can be found in all three states. It's very hard to prove to young students that gases exist at all! You can also divide materials into natural and artificial, in theory. Practically speaking, there is a continuum from natural materials such as rock, through worked and shaped materials, for example wood and slate; through changed materials such as glass and leather; to materials such as metals, most of which are not found in their pure state; to the totally artificial materials – synthetics such as plastics and artificial fibres. Finally, you can divide materials by use. Young students find this hard. It isn't always obvious why we choose certain materials for certain uses; glass for windows is one exception. Materials are sometimes used in direct contravention of their apparent purpose, e.g. furniture made of cardboard.

Explain — WS 23

Cloth or material?

Correct the key misconception that the word 'material' describes cloth. Also demonstrate that some objects can be made of materials that you might not expect. Point out that people wear plastic clothes, for example. They are sometimes made to look like a natural material like leather, but at a fraction of the cost.

What shall I be?

'Plastic' can imply that a material is soft and flexible. Some plastics are, but many are rigid and easily broken. The name relates to a stage in the shaping of the material when it is 'plastic' from the effects of heat. All plastics are fluid at some stage in their manufacture.

Scientifically, plastics can be put into one of two groups. Thermoplastics, such as polythene, PVC and polystyrene, are soft when warmed and harden as they cool. Thermosetting plastics, such as polyurethane and polyester, are rigid once set and don't soften when warmed.

Properties

Ask the students to list all the materials they can think of. Then ask them how they would recognize that material. Record a list of characteristics for reference in the activity, so students can identify the materials that objects around the school are made of. Students could complete WS 23 to consolidate their learning.

Things to do

All kinds of everything

The students will need to know a range of different materials and be able to broadly identify them. Suggest that they use the list from the starter activity to give them ideas.

Record

Lead the students on a 'treasure hunt' to record objects around the school and the materials they are made from.

Support

Some students might need help identifying the materials from which an object is made. Leave the list from the starter activity on the board to help them and limit the objects they have.

Extend

Ask students to count the number of objects made of a particular material and produce a bar chart of this information, identifying which material is most commonly used in the room.

Exploring

Remember that not all metals are magnetic. Iron and steel are, and so are cobalt and nickel and alloys of these. Some metal objects are misnamed. A food 'tin', for example, is commonly made of steel coated with a thin layer of tin, or of aluminium – like many soft drink cans. Some aluminium cans have a lid made of tin-coated steel.

Dig deeper

Students have the opportunity to find out more about 'precious' metals.

Did you know?

These facts show that the human body contains some strong materials.

I wonder...

Sometimes just looking isn't enough to decide if an object is made of a certain material. Plastic can be made to look like wood. The top of most modern desks in schools has a plastic wood-effect laminate. Sometimes it is made to look like marble or granite. The advantage of plastic is its versatility and durability compared to natural materials.

Other ideas

Wood or not?

Wood is a natural material, but can be a difficult topic to teach because of prior ideas held by students and some everyday uses of terminology.

Young students may regard mature trees as no more living than rocks and stones. Point out the seasonal changes in trees to demonstrate that they are living things.

Classifying trees into deciduous (leaf-shedding) and evergreen is easy, but the classification of hard and soft wood is confusing. It depends not on the density of the wood, but on the tree type; so 'hard woods' include balsa, for example.

Presentation

Ask the students to imagine they are groups of builders and to use PowerPoint to present their findings from the school survey. They could include photographs and any graphs they drew to show which materials were used most.

At home

WS 24

Ask the students to carry out a survey of materials used in their home, similar to the one they did around school, using WS 24. Let them compare the number of different materials in both places.

Plenary

Play a 'what's it made of?' game. Name an object and ask the students to say what material it is made from. Include items that can be made from different materials, e.g. tables.

Unit 3: Characteristics of materials – Using materials

The objectives for this lesson are that students should be able to:

- Explore how different materials have different properties

- Test materials to discover their properties

- Understand how knowing about properties helps us use materials in the best way

- Research people who have discovered new materials, such as John Wesley Hyatt.

SB pp.42–43 | *Starter*

- Show the students a picture of a person skiing. *What are their clothes made from? What are their skis made from? Why do you think these materials are good for these uses?*

- Show the students some of the materials they looked at in the last lesson. *Can you remember what this material is? How do you know?* Try to use materials themselves, as well as objects made of them. Discuss how the students recognized the materials. Were they correct? *Do you need to do some tests or make more observations to make sure you are right?*

Explain

Cutting edge

Knives were among the first tools invented by humans. There is evidence that they were the first utensils used for eating. Various materials have been used to make knives over time. Ask the students why a wooden knife may be used for butter but not for meat. Why do we sometimes use plastic knives that aren't very strong? They are light to carry on picnics and cheap to throw away if you don't want to wash up!

A chocolate saucepan

Illustrate this section by asking the students to hold a chocolate button in their hands and describe what happens.

⚠ Make sure the students wash their hands before you give them the chocolate and check for allergies, as you will have a hard job stopping them licking it off afterwards!

Things to do

What have you got?

Ask students to test a variety of materials. These can either be similar objects of different materials, or pieces of the materials used previously. The tests they need to do on each material include:

- touching it to see if it feels warm

- trying to bend it

- hitting it to see if it breaks easily

- hitting it to see if it rings

- seeing if it is shiny

- placing masses on top of it over a gap in the table (like a bridge) to see how strong it is

- holding it up to the light to see if it is transparent

- finding out if it soaks up liquid

- discovering if it lets heat pass through easily

- finding out if it is magnetic.

Record

Encourage students to use the correct terminology for materials and their properties, e.g. 'flexible' rather than 'bendy', 'transparent' rather than 'see-through'.

Support

Ensure that the pieces of metal are thin enough to bend or, if they are objects, show that they have already been bent. Two examples of the same material of different thicknesses might help.

Extend

Most students should be able to note down the properties of a particular material. Some will be able to use these properties to recognize a material and use the correct terminology, e.g. 'conductor', 'flexible', 'transparent'. Invite students to think of the uses of the materials they have looked at, based on the properties they have.

Biographies

John Wesley Hyatt discovered celluloid, an early plastic. It was used to make billiard balls. He mixed nitrocellulose with camphor and produced a white solid that could be moulded when warm and then set into shape.

Dig deeper

Students have the opportunity to find out more about the different kinds and uses of paper, such as writing paper.

Did you know?

These facts illustrate that materials sometimes have unexpected properties and are not always used as expected.

- Ancient Egyptians slept on stone pillows. The Japanese sleep on wooden pillows.

I wonder...

We often use polystyrene cups for hot drinks. They are thick to retain the heat.

Other ideas

Is it appropriate?

Ask the students to think of some other inappropriate uses of materials, e.g. lead balloons, chocolate fireguards, wooden saucepans, and explain their reasons. Let them illustrate their ideas and write an explanation underneath.

Happy families

Let the students make a set of cards with the materials' names on and another set with a separate card for each property that it has. They could play a game similar to 'Happy families'. The winner is the student holding a material and three of its properties, e.g. glass, hard, brittle, transparent.

Material riddle

Ask the students to play a game where one of them describes the properties of a material and the rest guess what the material is.

Presentation

Ask the students to research how the uses of materials have changed over time and prepare a presentation, in pairs, to show how a material is suited, or not, to its use. They could import pictures onto slides or use drawing packages to illustrate why the objects are good or bad at their job.

At home

WS 25

Ask the students to look at the labels in their clothes and to write down the materials that they are made of. Most clothes are made from a mixture of materials to combine the properties of each. What do they notice about clothes that are stretchy? (They normally contain elastic or Lycra.) Ask the students to complete WS 25 to consolidate their learning.

Plenary

List some objects on the board and ask the students what materials they could be made of and why. For example, spoons can be metal, plastic or wood; bags can be paper, plastic or leather.

New International Edition

Unit 3: Characteristics of materials – Building bridges

The objectives for this lesson are that students should be able to:

- Make predictions on which materials will be best for bridges
- Plan an experiment to investigate the best bridge-building materials
- Understand that experiments need to be fair
- Explain what they found out using their scientific knowledge.

Starter

SB pp.44–45

- Look around your locality for bridges – a pedestrian bridge across a motorway, a bridge linking two shopping centres, a footpath across a stream. *Where are they? Why are they there? What are they made from? Who uses them?* Emphasize that bridges are built for a purpose. *What would happen if the bridge was closed?*

- Show some photographs of bridges. *What important properties has the bridge got?* Discuss which materials they think have these properties. This will help when the students make a prediction in the enquiry to follow.

The challenge

Read the What to do and speech bubbles on page 44 in the *Student Book*. Discuss which material the students expect to be best for building bridges from the properties they have explored already. Ask them to predict. Encourage students to explain why they believe that material is best.

What to do

Set the students the problem of bridging a gap. The easiest is between two table tops. Show how folding or rolling paper can strengthen an otherwise weak material and then try these challenges. Limit the materials students use to a sheet of A4 paper, some paper clips, a length of clear tape for each bridge. Insist that the bridge is unattached to the tables. Ask that the bridges be designed and made to carry a particular mass – reasonable, but challenging. To make straight comparisons, ask that the test bridges be built side by side. Ask that the bridges be aesthetically pleasing, as well as relatively strong.

Students can make bridges of remarkable strength using newspapers and tape. Linked together, a number of rolled newspapers can be used to bridge wide gaps or take significant loads.

The bridges are best tested by hanging masses underneath. Attach a carrier bag and ask the students to put the masses in it.

The card will be the most difficult to monitor. It needs to be secured to the tables as it is not rigid. Fold it to make it the same thickness as the other materials. The students may realize that this isn't fair, and leave it unattached. This means that the first mass they try will end up on the floor!

> ⚠ Students will need to keep their toes well out of the way in case the masses fall on the floor. Place a box under the bridge to catch falling bags and masses.

What you need

- a selection of materials – plastic, wood, metal, paper, card and other classroom materials
- masses in carrier bags
- rulers
- sticky tape and paper clips
- digital camera or video camera
- digital microscope

What to check

Ensure that the tests are fair for each material. Keep the size of the materials the same. The size of the gap should be kept constant. Make sure that the masses are hung carefully.

Support

Some students may be very eager to just add extra masses and see the bridge collapse. Encourage them to count to ten before taking a result and then another ten before adding the next mass. Let them time ten seconds, so they are developing another skill.

Extend

Challenge the students to model an opening bridge. Tell them about raising bascule bridges and swing bridges, as well as bridges where the entire deck ascends like a lift. Which is the best solution to their challenge? Can they build it?

What did you find?
WS 26

Record

The students should use WS 26 to record the mass held by each material, then convert their recorded data into a chart. As a fallback, they could use the Young Engineers' data given in the *Student Book*. As the data in this enquiry is not continuous, only a bar chart can be produced that is consistent with the data.

Present

The bar chart will clearly show which material supported the most mass. Let the students use the chart to imagine they are presenting their results to a company of bridge builders, recommending which material they should use.

Can you do better?
WS 27

Show the students the Young Engineers' report from WS 27 and read it together. It is a good report. The students have made a prediction and attempted to explain where their prediction has come from. They have drawn and labelled a diagram and a table of their results, although a bar chart would help to interpret this. Their conclusion states not only which material was strongest, but also answers the title question of which material should be used for bridge building.

Encourage the students to talk about the experiment they have just done and how the material needs to be strong and stay straight. *What would happen if you repeated the experiment?*

Now predict

Students could gather and share their information on bridge materials and make predictions on other suitable materials for building.

Other ideas

Video

Record the addition of the masses so the students can watch how the material changes as the mass increases. If the tape is played back at double speed, the changes become more noticeable.

Digital microscope

Look at the materials both before and after they have had the masses added. *Do the materials look any different?* The students may notice small cracks appearing in rigid objects.

At home
WS 28

Ask the students to research famous bridges, and perhaps to 'adopt' one. What stories and legends are connected with their bridge? Students can also carry out the activity on WS 28.

Plenary

Remind students that materials are tested to find their properties. Give them a new material, e.g. a piece of elastic or ceramic, and ask them what sort of bridge it would make. The elastic will stretch too much, and the ceramic will break too easily and suddenly.

Unit 3: Characteristics of materials – Comparing materials

The objectives for this lesson are that students should be able to:

- Understand that some materials have similar properties

- Compare materials to see that some properties are more useful to us than others

- Find out that some materials can be recycled and used again

- Sort materials into groups based on their properties and usefulness.

SB pp.46–47 — Starter

- Show a picture of a stone house. *What are the walls made of? What about the roof?* Bring in a range of building materials, e.g. bricks, stones, mortar, cement and wood. *What do these building materials have in common? How are they different?* Ask the students to think about why houses used to be built from wood, but are now often made from stone. *What properties does stone have that makes it better for building houses?*

- Wear an aluminium-foil scarf or belt. *Do you like my new clothes? Is it a suitable material for clothes?* If you have some wooden clogs, wear them and discuss what property makes them suitable for shoes. They used to be mainly worn as outdoor shoes as they are waterproof.

Explain

Prime property

Let the students test various materials to lever open a small, empty paint tin. Give them a selection of metal, wood, paper, plastic and other materials. Make sure the materials are thin enough to go under the rim of the tin. Beware of breakages, especially splintered wood. Discuss which might be best and why before investigating the materials.

Produce a list of materials together and decide which property is the most important. This may vary according to the function, e.g. transparency is usually the most important property of glass, but very thin glass is used for medicine phials that need to be strong, but break open easily.

Something in common

Ask the students to think of properties that materials share and then explore how the different materials are used. Look back at the bridges: stone, metal and wood have been used to make bridges. All these materials share the property of strength.

Things to do — WS 29

Not as tough as boots

Start by showing the students some clothes with holes in, or ask them how they get holes in their clothes. Then ask students to rub blocks of wood over the surface of a variety of materials, such as tiles, bricks, fabric, paper, plastic. *Do you sometimes get holes in other materials?* Usually paper, after a lot of rubbing out!

Record

You can make a subjective judgement by holding the material up to the light, or measure the results with a light sensor. The more the material has worn, the more light will pass through it. The tile and opaque products should be the same before and after the test. Paper and fabric and some plastics may be thinner, so let more light through. The students can record their results on WS 29.

Support

Some students might need help to make the test fair, i.e. counting the number of rubs backwards and forwards and applying the same pressure and speed. Tell the students to count out loud and agree on whether a rub is one direction or both directions before they start.

Extend

Most students will be able to recognize that some materials don't wear as quickly as others. Ask them if they notice the wood or the material becoming warm. Encourage them to investigate different types of the same material, e.g. fabric or plastic, to observe the wear. They could relate this to the use of the type of material.

The students could survey the number of different kinds of plastic they use every day, e.g. bags, pens, remote controls, etc.

Dig deeper

Students have the opportunity to find out more about why plastic is better than wood and steel for some jobs.

Did you know?

These facts show students that some materials can be used again. Ask them what items their family recycles.

I wonder...

The students could look at the strength of the same thicknesses of paper and plastic bags and observe what they do when they are ripped or stretched. They could then compare the materials to the wrapper of a chocolate bar.

Other ideas

Best of all

Let the students do further comparison tests on materials for flexibility, transparency and conduction of heat. Help them to produce a ranking of the materials so they could then predict which material would be best for which job. Then set a design and technology task for the students to make an object of your choice, e.g. a tower, a bridge, a vase, a piece of cutlery. They should decide which material to use, using their experimental evidence.

Making plastic

If you want a more permanent plastic, you can make some from milk! Bring a flask of warm, not hot, full-cream milk into the classroom. Pour it into a bowl and add vinegar to it, preferably spirit vinegar; about a tablespoonful to half a pint (or 250 ml) of milk is right. Use a fine plastic kitchen sieve, or a cheese cloth, to sieve the resulting 'curds and whey'. Let the solid curds dry out a little. The result feels cheesy, but it can be shaped and left to dry further. It eventually becomes hard enough to keep, and will take paint and varnish.

You can make curious plastic fibres by squirting the full-cream milk from a plastic pipette into the pure vinegar. The strands that form have no great strength, but they are different from their constituent materials.

Presentation

Ask students to pretend to be crockery manufacturers, explaining which materials could be used for making a plate. They should then explain which one would be best and why.

At home

Ask the students to make a list of all the plastic items found in one room of their home. Could they be better made from another material? Why?

Plenary

Show a range of objects, similar to those used in the initial sorting activity. How would you sort the objects now? The students may want to categorize some objects more than once, so have a couple of objects made of the same material. This should illustrate that the students have progressed from sorting simple properties, e.g. colour and use, to thinking about the properties of the material, rather than the object.

Unit 3: Characteristics of materials – Exploring paper

The objectives for this lesson are that students should be able to:

- Discover which paper absorbs water fastest

- Plan and take part in a scientific experiment

- Develop methods of making their experiment fair

- Explain what they found out using their scientific knowledge.

SB pp.48–49   *Starter*

- Knock over a glass of water on your desk, then hunt around for something to mop it up with. Try any sort of material, including paper, e.g. tissues, toilet paper, paper towels. *Which sort of material should you have chosen? Why? What is the property of paper that mops up the water?*

- Show a range of different types of paper. *Can you see the fibres? What are they used for?* Let the students look at some papers through a microscope to see the differences to help them decide. This should illustrate that the same material can not only share properties, but can have different properties that are sometimes more important.

The challenge

Read the What to do and conversation on page 48 in the *Student Book*. Discuss the problem of needing to clear up the mess very quickly. Is the amount of liquid spilled important? Does it matter how much paper you use to clear up the spill?

What to do

The challenge is to find a type of paper that will clean up a liquid spill as quickly as possible. All the suggestions given are useable, but only the third option will work for all the pieces of paper, as some of the pieces of paper will not absorb all the liquid, no matter how long you give them! The volume of liquid will need to be measured to ensure that each paper has the same amount of liquid to absorb. Once the paper has been placed in the water (which you can colour to make it easier to see), start the stopwatch to time 1 minute. You will see that the paper that absorbs fastest will draw the water furthest up.

This is not a measure of how much water the paper will absorb.

This is called capillary action. Capillarity is also used by plants to draw the water up the stem, as in the experiment in Unit 2.

What you need

- different types of paper, all cut to the same length and width

- stopwatches

- beakers to measure and hold water in

- food colouring to colour water

- rulers

- digital camera or video camera

What to check

To ensure a fair test, the pieces of paper all need to be the same size. The volume of water should also be the same, as should the time to absorb the liquid.

By measuring how far the water has travelled up the paper, the students should be able to work out which one is best for clearing up the spill.

> ⚠ Spills can cause accidents. Teach students to mop up spills immediately.

Support

Make sure students hold the paper upright throughout the minute, but check that the end stays in the water! You might need to help some students to measure the height of the water on the paper.

Extend

All students should be able to observe which paper carries the water up further. Some students will be able to measure accurately. Some students could test a range of the same paper type but from different manufacturers. They could also investigate whether the type of liquid being absorbed makes a difference.

What did you find?   WS 30

Record

The students should use WS 30 to summarize their evidence and produce a graph. If their results are inconclusive, they could use the data given in the *Student Book*. The data in this enquiry is not continuous so only a bar graph can be produced that is consistent with the data.

Present

Invite the students to imagine that they work for a paper manufacturer and to produce a marketing campaign on the best type of paper to clean up wet spills. If they use a digital camera to take pictures of the water being absorbed by the paper, these could be imported into a PowerPoint presentation.

Can you do better?
WS 31

Show the students the SuperSoak kitchen roll report from WS 31 and read it together. Was the conclusion correct? *Did the manufacturer test enough different types of paper? If you test different brands of the same type of paper, does it make a difference?* Point out to the students that manufacturers would have us believe it did, hence their advertising campaigns. Ask the students to suggest some experiments to test different brands of paper and also to look at whether the type of liquid used is important. *If we spill golden syrup, will the paper that absorbs water absorb this too?*

Now predict

Shiny, thin paper will repel water the most. Some students will already have experienced their textbook coming into contact with a wet surface. Usually the ink runs as well. The students should refer back to the results of their experiment to see which paper was least effective at absorbing liquid.

Other ideas

Paper making

The students could try to make their own paper and test it for absorbency. Let them shred some paper and mix it with water into a pulp. Spread the pulp onto a cooling rack or gauze and leave it to dry. Rolling the damp paper with a rolling pin will make it even thinner. Let the students try making paper of different thicknesses and then predict which will be most absorbent.

Branded

Let the students test different brands of kitchen roll to see which manufacturers' claims are valid.

At home
WS 32

The students may be horrified to learn that people have used newspaper as toilet paper! Would it have been any good? Ask the students to look at the structure of newspaper and to test its absorbency. How well does it absorb water? Can you think of another problem with using printed newspaper? WS 32 allows students to investigate the strength of paper.

Plenary

Look at some other types of paper, e.g. sandpaper, paper made from hemp (also made into ropes), manila envelopes, jute paper sacks, and money made from cotton rags. Why do these types of paper have a particular use? Instead of being absorbent, these papers are tough and can't be torn very easily.

69

Unit 3: Characteristics of materials – Stretchy materials

The objectives for this lesson are that students should be able to:

- Discover why clothes need to be different sizes
- Find out that some materials stretch more than others
- Plan and take part in a scientific experiment
- Present their findings in a graph.

SB pp.50–51 | *Starter*

- Come in with a pair of very large socks if you can. Ask the students if they will fit you. They are obviously too big. They have been stretched. *Who will they fit?* Show some baby socks. *Who will they fit?* Some clothes stretch to fit.

- Bring in a piece of stretchy clothing such as a hat. It says on the label, 'one size fits all'. *Is this true?*

The challenge

Read the conversation on page 50 in the *Student Book* and discuss the dilemma with the students. Show some pairs of socks and let the students feel their thickness. They could also examine them under a hand lens to see what they look like. This will help with a prediction such as 'I think the socks with the bigger holes in will stretch most.' This quality is called the weave of the material.

The challenge involves finding the pair of socks that will stretch the most, so Bushra's grandma can wear them. The students will need to decide in which direction they are going to test the stretch, i.e. the length or the width. Does it make any difference?

What to do

You will need something to hang the socks from. One student could hold the socks in the air. A more reliable idea is to use G-clamps. The students put the mass in the socks. The lower to the ground this is carried out, the safer it is, avoiding the masses dropping on the floor from a great height.

What you need

- various pairs of socks of different types (try a range of different thicknesses and different brands)

- 500 g masses or 500 g made up from several masses
- rulers

What to check | WS 33

If the students are measuring how much the socks stretch, they will be looking at the difference in length between the stretched and unstretched socks. This involves a simple subtraction sum. Alternatively, they could hold a strip of paper behind the sock, mark its unstretched length, add the mass, mark the stretched length, and measure the distance between the two.

> ⚠️ Beware of falling masses on toes! Make sure the students stand well back, or have a box under the masses to make sure they don't land on feet. Limit the amount of mass per sock to 1 kg.

Support

Show the students how to measure accurately and how to record on a two-column table as on page 51 in the *Student Book*. This will produce a set of results similar to the *Student Book*.

Extend

Students should be able to predict which pair of socks will stretch the most from their thickness. Some students will be able to relate the amount of extension to the weave of the material and give a pattern of results, e.g. the thicker the socks, the less they stretch.

Some students could add more masses and measure the extension of the socks after each mass has been added. This will produce a more comprehensive set of results. Let them record their findings on WS 33.

What did you find? | WS 34

Record

The students could convert their recorded data from WS 33 into a graph on WS 34. If their data is inconclusive, they can use the idealized data given in the *Student Book* and on WS 34. If the students plot a graph of thickness against stretch, they can produce a line graph, since the data is continuous, i.e. the thicker the socks, the less they stretch.

Present

The students will need to use the graph to explain what they found out. They could present the experiment to the rest of the class and use their graph to predict the appearance and stretchiness of an untested pair of socks.

Can you do better?

Show the students Bushra's diary from WS 34 and read it together.

The report is a bit brief. There is no attempt at an explanation in the prediction. *The fair test is not complete, so was the experiment fair? A line graph could have been drawn of the results, but would this tell you any more?* Bushra has not explained the pattern of her results, only which ones she would give to her grandma.

Now predict

A comparison of Lycra and non-Lycra clothes should show that the ones with Lycra are more stretchy, and also recover their shape better after being stretched.

Other ideas

Testing other fabrics

Strips of other fabrics can be cut and tested to give students more experience of testing stretch. The practical problem is gripping the fabric. A G-clamp will hold the top of the fabric, of course, but you may need to grip the bottom of the strip with a bulldog clip and hang weights from that. You could put them in a carrier bag. As before, beware of masses falling on toes. Stand well back, or have a box under the masses to make sure they don't bounce on feet. Limit the amount of mass per bag to 1 kg.

At home

Ask the students to survey their clothes at home and to look at labels. *Which clothes stretch? What are they made of?*

Plenary

Show the students some new and untested socks. Pass them round and ask their opinions, as sock experts, on how well they are likely to stretch.

New International Edition

Unit 3: Characteristics of materials – Unit 3: Review

The objectives for this lesson are that students should be able to:

- Check what they have learned about the characteristics of materials in this Unit

- Find out how they are working within the Grade 3 level.

SB p.52 *Expectations*

Students working towards Grade 3 level will:

- Identify uses of some common materials

- Name some of the properties of a range of common materials

- Make measurements of length using standard units.

In addition, students working within Grade 3 level will:

- Suggest several reasons why the material is suitable for its job

- Sort materials in terms of their properties

- Identify that a material can do a range of jobs

- Explain it is important to test materials to find out whether descriptions of characteristics are reliable

- Recognize when a test or comparison is unfair.

Further to this, students working beyond Grade 3 level will also:

- Explain how to make a test fair

- Represent measurements in a bar chart.

Check-up

As the hutch will stay outside all year, it must be weatherproof. This means any material that is not waterproof is not a sensible option. Plastic could work, but it would need to be the kind that doesn't change with heat and that would resist rabbit teeth! It also needs to be strong enough to be flexible. Wood is waterproof and strong. Rubber would be too stretchy. Glass would be impractical. How easy is the material to keep clean?

Assessment WS 35

Use the Unit 3 assessment on WS 35 to check the students' understanding of the content of the Unit. The answers are given opposite.

Name: _____ Date: _____

WS 35 Unit 3 assessment

1 Look at this picture of a house.

Windows are made of

is made of tiles.

Walls are made of

Doors are made of plastic or

a) Finish labelling the house.
b) Why use bricks for walls?
_____
c) Why is glass used for windows?
_____
d) Why do tiles make a good roof?
_____

2 a) What material would you stir boiling water with?
_____
b) Why?
_____

Unit 3: Characteristics of materials   35

Answers

1 **a** Windows are made of **glass**.
The **roof** is made of tiles.
Walls are made of **brick**, concrete or wood.
Doors are made of plastic or **wood**.

   b A brick is hard and strong.

   c Glass is transparent, strong, hard, not flexible and waterproof. It's transparent so it lets light into the house. It's strong/ hard/not flexible so it stays in place. It's waterproof so it doesn't let rain into the house. (Any of these answers with reasons.)

   d Slate is waterproof.

2 **a** Any material that doesn't conduct heat and doesn't melt in boiling water can be used, e.g. wood.

   b So that it doesn't conduct heat (easily) and you don't get burned (feel the heat).

The answer!

Refer back to the introductory question. Rubber is waterproof, flexible and hard-wearing. It can be moulded to the shape of a wheel or a foot. It wears slowly, but its characteristics don't change. It can hold air at high pressure in car and bike tyres. Car tyres are more likely to cover greater distances than feet and so they must be thicker than shoe soles to last longer!

And finally...

Display a range of materials with a card next to each one stating its uses and properties. Leave it for other students to see. A hands-on display is even better, so include some examples of socks and ask the students to touch them. Also, set up some materials under a microscope for them to observe.

Let the students investigate how fabrics are made for clothes, e.g. look at wool weaving or twisting.

New International Edition

Unit 4: Rocks and soils

The objectives for this Unit are that students should be able to:

- Discover that rock is beneath the surface of the Earth

- Learn to recognize rocks and their characteristics

- Find out what different soils are made up of

- Make predictions that they prove by finding evidence.

SB p.53   Science background

From the highest mountain to the deepest ocean trench, our Earth is a rocky planet. There are thousands of different rocks and minerals on and in the Earth. In its four and a half billion-year-old history, these rocks have been worn away by weather, plants and animals, changed, and reformed into new and different kinds of rocks and soils. Rock-forming and rock-eroding processes are constantly active. As they recycle the rocks, these processes help form the landscape we see today.

The best way of learning about rocks is to look closely at as many as you can find – pebbles on the beach or stones from the garden are as good a starting point as professional mineral sets. Students should be recognizing common rocks and their uses, using language associated with size (stone, pebble, grain, etc.) and recognizing characteristics such as colour, texture, hardness, permeability and drainage.

Language

Crust	The surface layer of the Earth.
Minerals	Naturally occurring chemicals in rocks.
Igneous	'Of fire' – rocks that are formed from molten rock.
Sedimentary	Rocks laid down in layers – usually by water, but sometimes by wind or ice.
Metamorphic	'Changed' rocks that have been changed by temperature or pressure.
Permeable	A material which allows water through easily.
Humus	Soil that is largely made from decaying plant matter.

Cement	An artificial rock substitute made by heating a mixture of crushed limestone and clay. It sets when mixed with sand and water.

The Words to learn list on page 53 of the *Student Book* can be used to make a classroom display.

Resources

- *Rocks and Soils* Reader.

- A selection of rocks.

- A selection of soils and soil materials – sand, clay, peat.

- Funnels, beakers and measuring cylinders.

- Magnifying lenses.

- Soft cloth.

- Sieves with different-sized holes.

- Seconds timer.

- Rulers.

- Soft paper.

- Reference books on rocks and minerals.

- pH indicator strips.

- Shoes encrusted with different soils.

Bright ideas

It's often quite difficult to find enough natural soils in one locality to provide a range for students to experiment with. Short of filling the boot of your car with soil every time you drive to a different location, one solution is to manufacture a range of soil types artificially from components found in garden centres. They will sell you various potting composts, sand, lime and gravel from which you can make up your own soil recipes.

Knowledge check

- Students should recognize that rocks are naturally occurring materials.

- Students should know that there is rock under all surfaces.

- Students should understand that different rocks have different properties.

- Students should understand that soils come from rocks.

74

- Students should know that soil is formed from small particles of rock and decaying organic material.
- Students should understand that the characteristics of a soil depend upon the characteristics of the rock from which it was formed.
- Students may believe that soil is the same everywhere, whereas it may vary considerably even within the same garden.

> ⚠ Warn students that soil (particularly if taken from a garden) will contain bacteria and chemicals. They should wash their hands after handling soil. Some minerals can be poisonous, so students should not put rocks in their mouths.

Skills check

Students need to:

- make careful observations and measurements
- collect evidence and decide how good it is
- use their evidence to explain what they found out
- measure time and volumes of water with accuracy.

Some students will:

- be able to explain what their investigations and experiments show in terms of the characteristics and uses of the rocks and soils tested.

Links to other subjects

Literacy: Using descriptive language to compare and describe rocks. Investigating the etymology of words in Earth Science such as 'metamorphic', 'geology', etc. Investigating interesting suffixes, e.g. 'ology', 'ite', 'ous', etc. *Ug* by Raymond Briggs is a lovely story about a student from the Stone Age and his quest for comfortable trousers.

Numeracy: Measuring and comparing using standard units. Organizing and interpreting simple data in bar graphs and tables. Measuring volume.

ICT: Using a multimedia package to combine text and graphics to make a presentation. Using spreadsheets to record and analyze data. Using branching databases to identify rocks, minerals and soils.

Geography: Researching and investigating plate tectonics, volcanoes and earthquakes. Work could also incorporate aspects of weathering and erosion and how this affects the landscape.

Art: Looking at the ancient rock art of Australia or the cave paintings of Lascaux. Investigating how painters in the past made pigments from ground-up rocks and minerals.

History: Finding out how archaeologists use the colour and composition of soil to help them locate ancient sites.

Let's find out...

The Unit opens with this question:

> Eshwar's family has just moved to a new house with a lovely garden, but Eshwar's dad isn't very happy. 'This soil is waterlogged. It is heavy clay. It'll take a lot of work before I can grow much in here,' he grumbled. What must Eshwar's dad do to change the soil?

Discuss the problem with the students and encourage them to suggest solutions. What does your own garden, or the school garden, look like? Can we always see the soil? Encourage the students to use as wide a vocabulary as possible, and use this as an opportunity to explore the subtleties of descriptive language and the need for precise observations in science.

Unit 4: Rocks and soils – Types of rock

The objectives for this lesson are that students should be able to:

- Find out some of the different ways that rocks are formed

- Discover some of the uses for rocks

- Learn how rocks are classified into one of three main types

- Safely make edible 'rocks' to represent these three main types.

SB pp.54–55

Starter

- Display a photograph of a seashore. *What can you see? Do you think that the rocks stop where the sea meets the land?*

- Display a photograph of a volcano. *What does this volcano have in common with the seashore scene?* The forces in the Earth that created the volcano were the same forces that created the pebbles on the beach.

Explain

The Earth

The Earth, Sun and other planets were created from a cloud of dust and gas. As the cosmic dust was squeezed together, the Earth formed into a giant molten sphere. Four and a half billion years later, the Earth's core is still cooling down! The surface of the Earth is cold and rocky; the inside, however, is a mass of red-hot liquid rock that sometimes spurts to the surface in volcanic eruptions.

The surface of the Earth is split into huge pieces called tectonic plates. These plates fit together like a jigsaw but are constantly moving. Demonstrate this by peeling an orange and trying to fit the pieces back together around the fruit. Where the peel meets are the edges of the plates or boundaries where volcanoes and earthquakes are most common.

What's in a rock?

A mineral can be defined as any non-organic substance that can be dug out from the ground. Rocks are made of minerals.

Limestone and coal can reveal remnants of organic remains such as fossil shells. Granite is made from feldspar (which can be grey or pink-coloured), mica (which is grey/black) and quartz (clear and glass-like).

Uses of rock

Students may be familiar with Stone Age tools or flint arrow heads, and with ancient monuments such as the Egyptian pyramids. Rock is generally heavy and difficult to transport, so local buildings are likely to be made of locally available stone.

Other uses of rocks (and minerals) may be less obvious. Quartz is used in silicon chips to make computers, clocks and watches work. Fluorite and chalk are used in toothpaste. Talc is used as a cosmetic. Pumice, a volcanic rock, is used as a cosmetic abrasive. Gunpowder is made from the mineral saltpetre, diamonds are used in dentists' drills, and of course we use salt to flavour foods.

Things to do

Rock feast

Scientists classify rocks into three main types according to how they were formed. These cooking activities should illustrate the different methods of formation and some of the visual characteristics the students can pick out in rock samples.

Igneous: Igneous rocks are formed when molten rock is forced up from inside the Earth. Volcanic rocks (such as basalt, obsidian and pumice) cool quickly and have small crystals, whereas plutonic rocks (such as granite and dolerite) are slow to cool and have larger crystals. (When molten rock is under the ground we call it magma, and lava when it reaches the surface.)

Sedimentary: These are really new rocks from old and are made of layers of small particles or sediments from other rocks. These sediments, washed down in streams and rivers, settle in layers where they combine with plant and animal debris. Sedimentary rocks such as shale, limestone and sandstone are those in which you are most likely to find fossils.

Another common type of sedimentary rock is called a conglomerate, an example of which is called 'puddingstone'. Here, larger pebbles are squeezed and cemented together to form a lumpy mess.

Metamorphic: These are igneous or sedimentary rocks that have been changed under the Earth's crust by heat and pressure into something new, e.g. slate, marble, gneiss.

Record

Make a class display of a rock lunch box or picnic with the real rocks linked to the fun food rocks. *How was each made and what characteristics do they share?*

Support

Encourage students to feel the rock samples and think about how the texture, shape and appearance of each one relates to its formation. Limit your samples to just one or two of each type and encourage the use of descriptive language.

Extend

Encourage the students to look for clues in the rocks to find out how they were formed, e.g. the stratification layers of sedimentary rocks or the frothy appearance of volcanic ones. Streaks of coloured minerals are characteristic of marble.

Fossil hunter

The tongue-twister 'She sells seashells on the seashore' is reputedly linked to the pioneer palaeontologist Mary Anning, who lived in the early nineteenth century in Lyme Regis, Dorset, UK.

Did you know?

These facts will illustrate the power of the Earth to students.

I wonder...

The movement of the Earth's crust causes earthquakes. When plates either push against each other or pull apart, pressure builds up in the rocks on either side of the cracks. Too much pressure and the rocks will jerk – that's when an earthquake happens.

Other ideas

Make a fossil

Let the students press a shell, leaf or flower into a block of modelling clay to make a mould. Put the mould into a plastic tub and cover it with liquid plaster of Paris. Leave it to set overnight and let the students remove the modelling clay to reveal their new 'fossil' – a cast of the original!

Chemical volcanoes

Attach a card cone around a small bottle containing bicarbonate of soda. Add vinegar and red food colouring and watch your frothy lava pour out.

ICT ideas

Use a drawing program to create a repeating pattern based on rocks or fossils to use as desktop wallpaper or to print out as a greetings card or wrapping paper.

Presentation

Make a collage display of uses of rocks using pictures from magazines and catalogues.

Ask the students to prepare a PowerPoint presentation, explaining how many different types of rock are useful to us.

At home   WS 36   WS 37

Students can use WS 36 to make rock cakes at home.

Encourage them to go to their bathroom and identify the different rocks they find there. Ask the students to complete WS 37.

Plenary

Give each student a rock identity such as chalk, granite or sandstone, or ask them to choose their own rock or gemstone. Ask them to describe the rock's properties to the class.

Unit 4: Rocks and soils – Sorting rocks

The objectives for this lesson are that students should be able to:

- Remember facts about how rocks are formed
- Discover how to classify rocks by the way they look
- Make a branching key to identify a collection of rocks
- Learn that there can be 'odd ones out' when things are grouped.

SB pp.56–57 — Starter

- Revise what the students have discovered so far about how rocks are formed.
- Play a 'fact or fib' game. Post two signs labelled 'fact' and 'fib' around the room. Read out statements related to work so far. Challenge students to decide whether each statement is a fact or a fib and go to the correct sign.
- Explain that rocks are formed in different ways and they look and feel different. Show some rocks and describe their appearance in terms of colour, particle or grain size, roughness or smoothness, how the colour is distributed (uniformly or in speckles or blotches), whether the rocks are hard or crumbly and so on. Some of your rocks may be a mixture of different rocks stuck together.

The challenge

Read the conversation on page 56 of the *Student Book* and explain that Uncle Omar was a geologist who studied the Earth's crust. Discuss how Layla and Ali might begin to sort out the rocks. Make a list of possibilities on the board.

What to do

Give groups of students some rocks to examine. Encourage them to use hand lenses and to use as wide a descriptive vocabulary as possible.

What you need

- a selection of rocks
- hand lenses
- reference books and field guides on rocks and minerals

What to check

Students will have to make some very careful observations in this enquiry. Some students will not be satisfied just sorting rocks into groups and will demand to know their names and origins. Most of the rocks contained in a mineral set will be identified by the supplier but if you have an old set with the labels missing, or if you are using rocks you have found, the identification may be more difficult. Students can become frustrated if you don't have a 'right answer' to hand so prepare yourself in advance. Keep it simple. Generally, the most obvious match is the correct one.

Support

Restrict the numbers of samples and encourage students to sort into only two groups. Colour is an easy one to start with and your categories could be as simple as 'white/not white'. This 'yes/no' grouping technique must be grasped securely in preparation for devising branching keys.

Extend

All students should be able to devise at least two groupings; more able students may find more, or more interesting groupings, for example based on particle size or texture. Encourage these students to use secondary sources to name and group their samples. They should try to find at least two or three ways to group their collection.

What did you find?   WS 38

Record

Students can use WS 38 to record the different ways they grouped their rocks. Encourage students to give descriptive names to their groups. Be prepared for the inevitable, 'We like the ones in this group, but not the ones in this group!'

Look at Ali and Layla's table. The headings for their groups are Igneous, Sedimentary and Metamorphic. Ali and Layla must therefore have moved sandstone into Group 2 as it is a sedimentary, not an igneous rock.

Present

Encourage the students to make displays of their rocks sorted into groups. There may be disagreements, but there are no 'right answers' to this activity. What the students should be able to do, however, is justify their choices based upon the characteristics they have observed. Make sure the students record their reasons for putting things into sets, e.g. 'has large particles/has small particles'.

Can you do better?

WS 39

Read through Ali's postcard on WS 39 with the students. Do you agree with the way he sorted out the rocks? Can you think of a different way to sort them?

The students are asked to make a key to identify their collection of rocks. Doing this with only paper and pencil is quite challenging. Encourage students to sort and label their collection by moving the samples themselves and linking them with ribbon or paper strips so that they can see the specimen rather than just the name.

Now predict

Adding a mystery item to the collection is a way to test how well the students' categories stand up. It may be that they wish to change their final selection, or end up putting the rock into two separate categories. How well does this rock fit into their identification key? This helps practise the skills of close observation, discussing, questioning and classifying.

Other ideas

Who am I?

Play a '20 questions' guessing game, where the students match rock samples to the one you're thinking of. Also, play a variation of a memory game – let the students look at a tray of rocks or gemstones for 30 seconds, then cover the tray with a cloth. Without the students looking, remove one of the rocks and then take off the cloth. Can the students identify from memory alone which rock is missing? Students are often fascinated by the strange and unusual names of rocks and minerals; old-fashioned games like hangman are ideal for familiarizing students with the language of geology and generating questions requiring a yes/no answer.

ICT ideas

Use a branching key database to classify your rocks and build up a key. (These are variously known as tree databases, dichotomous keys or binary key programs – they're all the same thing.) This works best if the students have practised creating yes/no questions with something more familiar to them than rocks to begin with, e.g. groups of students in their class, different types of shapes or sweets.

At home

Ask the students to make a collection of boulder buddies. If the shape of a stone reminds them of a face or an animal or fish, ask them to wash and paint it to look more like one and then varnish it when it is dry.

Plenary

Students were asked to make judgements based upon observation. Discuss whether they think this is the best way group their rocks. They may now conclude that grouping on appearance may not be the only way. This leads nicely into the next activity.

Unit 4: Rocks and soils – Hard rocks

The objectives for this lesson are that students should be able to:

- Learn that some rocks are harder than others

- Find out which of their rocks are the hardest

- Develop methods of making their experiment fair

- Compare their own experiment and results to Layla and Ali's.

SB pp.58–59

Starter

- Find some fake diamond jewellery and wear it – children's dressing-up kits are good sources. Exaggerate how wonderful your jewels are until one of the students inevitably tells you that they aren't real. *How do you know? Can we ever really tell just by looking?*

- Explain that the word 'diamond' comes from the Greek word 'adamas', which means hardest metal. It is the hardest mineral we know and will scratch all other rocks. Your fake diamonds may be obvious copies but other fakes are more realistic. One way of telling good fakes from real diamonds is to do a scratch test.

The challenge

Read the conversation on page 58 in the *Student Book*. Discuss the children's ideas. *Can rocks float?* Remember that some rocks, such as pumice, have holes in them where gases were trapped during their formation; in fact, pumice floats. Pumice stone is used to rub down hard skin. Many rocks will soak up water or let water permeate through them.

Try any or all of Layla and Ali's ideas. Geologists would do all of these tests, and more, before identifying a rock. Geologists consider the colour of a sample, its lustre (what the surface looks like in the light), the specific gravity (how many more times the rock weighs compared to water), the cleavage of the rock (the pattern in which it breaks), its texture, the size and shape of the crystals, what colour streak the rock leaves on a surface and one of the most common tests, which is for hardness.

What to do

This test is really more accurately described as 'resistance to abrasion' rather than hardness, but it follows the 'hardness scale' published in 1882 by Frederick Mohs. Some rocks are soft enough to be scratched by your fingernail, others by a copper coin or a steel nail file. The principle behind this scale is that a harder rock will scratch a softer one.

What you need

- a selection of rocks

- a soft cloth

What to check

The students need to decide how they know when their rock has been scratched. Wiping with a cloth will remove any debris from a soft rock and the students should be looking for a definite scratch mark.

Support

Discuss how to make the test fair. Limit the number of rocks to three or four samples where the results will be obvious. Once the students have decided on their hardness scale, reinforce this by testing again with your fingernail, a coin and a steel file. *Are there any rocks that will be scratched by all the others? Are there any rocks that won't be scratched at all?*

Extend

Let the students explore a wider range of samples or other methods of testing such as permeability. *Are the hardest rocks the most waterproof?*

What did you find?

WS 40

Record

The students can use the table provided on WS 40 to record their results. The students could convert their data into a hardness scale. Less able students can present their results visually by lining up the actual rocks from softest to hardest.

Present

Ask the students to write about what they did. Encourage them to relate the softness or hardness of a rock to how easily the rocks are worn away. Students should be able to make statements relating hardness to use, e.g. 'The granite was hard so it could be used for roads or buildings, but the gypsum was very soft so it would wear down quickly.'

Can you do better?

WS
41

Ask students to review how good their evidence was using WS 41. How would they tackle the investigation differently if they were starting again?

The students are asked to find out about the Mohs scale, which is a 10-point scale of mineral hardness with the highest numbers being the hardest. Each mineral can scratch those with a lower number. *How does your rock scale compare to the Mohs scale?*

As a guide, your fingernail has a hardness of about 2.5 (somewhere between gypsum and calcite), a copper coin is about 3.5 and a steel file is around 7 on the Mohs scale, equal to the hardness of quartz.

Now predict

Softer rocks are made up of larger grains. There is space between the grains for water to enter. So these rocks are permeable – they absorb water.

To test for permeability, students could drip small quantities of water onto the rocks with a plastic pipette and observe how quickly (or not) it is absorbed.

Other ideas

Scratch art

Diamond is the hardest mineral we know. Glass cutters use diamond-tipped tools to cut and etch glass. Real etchings are difficult to do but you can use the tip of a steel nail to scratch into special black-coated metallic card to make patterns or a picture. Alternatively, let the students cover a sheet of paper with wax crayon as a colourful base, cover this over with a thick layer of black paint or ink and scratch a drawing into it.

At home

Ask the students to find examples in their neighbourhood where rocks have been weathered or eroded. Old buildings, for example, may have weathered statues outside them. The students may be able to see where stone steps have been worn away by thousands of pairs of feet over the centuries.

Plenary

Even the hardest rocks can be attacked and damaged by the weather, plants and animals. Weathering is when rocks are broken down by the forces of nature, e.g. by water freezing in a crack, forcing it open; by chemicals in acid rain dissolving limestone; or by biological weathering, which is caused by the roots of trees splitting rocks or by animals burrowing. Erosion, on the other hand, is the movement of rocks by rivers or glaciers or by the wind. Weathered rocks are more easily eroded. These tiny, broken-off bits of rock create sediment to make new rocks and also to make soil.

Unit 4: Rocks and soils – Types of soil

The objectives for this lesson are that students should be able to:

- Understand that soil covers much of the rocky surface of the Earth

- Learn what soil is made from

- Separate and sort soil particles using water

- Find out what farmers can do to make their soil more fertile.

SB pp.60–61 — *Starter*

- Bring in a large stone and some soil. Explain that the soil is made from rock like the one in front of them. *How do you think that happened?*

- Tell the students that they are going to discover how soil is made and what's in it.

Explain

Wearing down

Demonstrate the action of movement breaking down rocks by placing some sugar cubes in a sealed jam jar. Shake the jar. Sugar crystals will break off from the main lumps. Explain that this is one way that rocks can be broken down.

Now take a sugar cube and drop water on it; it starts to dissolve and fall apart. Tell the students that the chemicals dissolved in rainwater can attack some rocks in a similar way.

Try dripping vinegar onto a piece of chalk or limestone from a plastic pipette and watch it fizz as the acid eats away at the surface. Placing a seashell (formed mainly of calcium carbonate) in a jar of vinegar for a few days will reduce it to a crumbly mass in the same way. Caves are usually found in limestone areas where rainwater and carbonic acid have eaten away at the stone to form networks of tunnels and caverns.

Fertile land

Empty a handful of soil onto a large sheet of white paper and let the students examine it carefully. *What does it look like/feel like/smell like?* The students may be able to feel the gritty particles of rock in the soil or see plant debris or even small creatures. They might also feel that the soil is

damp. Water and air are important to the fertility of the soil.

> ⚠ Make sure the students always wash their hands thoroughly after handling soil.

In profile

If you dug a deep enough hole in soil, you'd probably come across three distinct layers of material. The first, topsoil, is the fertile layer we use for planting. It can be between a few centimetres and a few metres thick. Next, the subsoil has larger pieces of rock and very little plant debris. Finally, the bedrock has the parent material from which the majority of soil is made. Together, these three layers form the soil profile. Depending on the original bedrock and the proportions of other ingredients, your soil will be a unique mixture.

Things to do — WS 42

Analyze some soil

It is possible to sort out the various sizes of particles in soil, but it is much easier to separate them using water. The heaviest pebbles and soil particles will sink first, followed by the lighter particles. Plant material will float at the top of the jar. Look for air bubbles rising from the soil when you add the water. Air is needed to support the animal life within the soil.

Record

Students could draw the different layers they have discovered in their samples on WS 42.

Support

Students can sieve soil samples to remove progressively smaller particles. Let the students use several sieves with different mesh sizes and remind them to use the ones with the largest holes first.

Extend

Compare two or more soil samples. *What are the differences and the similarities? Are two samples from the same field identical? If not, why not?*

Dig deeper

Students have the opportunity to find out more about how farmers can make their soil more fertile.

Did you know?

Discuss the facts and encourage students to think about how we use rocks and soils.

- As new soil is formed over the centuries, it covers over the previous layers. Archaeologists know that the older something is, the deeper it is likely to be buried.

I wonder…

The garden is clearly better at draining than the field. It may be that the field is a more clay soil with the associated finer particles and small air spaces that make drainage difficult. The garden may be a freer-draining loam soil with a good mix of plant material and larger, grittier sand particles that would produce larger air spaces and faster drainage.

Other ideas

Cave chemistry

The build-up of cave formations in limestone caves (stala**g**mites rise from the **g**round and stala**c**tites hang from the **c**eiling) can take hundreds of years, but you can make something similar in just a few days! Fill two jars with a saturated solution of washing soda and suspend a 'rope' of twisted J-cloth between the two, making sure the ends of the cloth are well immersed in the soda solution. Put a dish under the centre of the cloth to catch the drips. As the water evaporates, your crystal pillars will grow. Keep the jars topped up with solution. Washing soda or alum works best, but you can get acceptable results using rock salt.

Acid showers

How pure is your rainwater? If you have a rainy season, test the drops using pH indicator paper to show the amount of acid in the water. Try to collect the water in jars or just stand in the rain! It's best not to use rain that has been standing in puddles because the acid content may be from the ground rather than the water. Pure water has a pH value of 7: anything above this is alkaline; below 7 is acidic. Expect unpolluted rainwater in towns to have a value of around 5.5, mildly acidic.

Presentation

Ask the students to pretend that they are a soil and write their autobiography. *How did you begin your life? What rock were you to begin with? How were you broken down? How did you come to be in this field or garden? Which other particles surround you? Who lives in you? What are you used for?*

At home

WS
43

Give students a small piece of sandstone or pumice to take home. Ask them to soak each rock in water for a few hours and then put it in a small plastic bag. Keep the rock in a freezer overnight and then thaw it out the next day. *Have any small particles broken off?* Ask students to complete WS 43 to consolidate their learning.

Plenary

When is a rock not a rock? When it's a pebble or a stone or sand or soil! The transition from rock to soil is long and involves several stages. At each stage, the size of the particle acquires a new name. Use this as an opportunity to sort a selection of rocks and stones, pebbles, gravel and boulders into size order. Reinforce the fact that, even though they are different sizes and have different names, they are all made of rock.

New International Edition

Unit 4: Rocks and soils – Testing soils

The objectives for this lesson are that students should be able to:

- Recognize that each soil shows a different set of characteristics

- Carry out an experiment to find out which soil is which

- Examine evidence from other students' results

- Reflect on how they could make their own experiments better.

SB pp.62–63

Starter

- Dress yourself as a 'soil detective' if appropriate – a soil-streaked lab coat would be ideal. Explain to the students that a dreadful thing has happened. Some thoughtless teacher has walked across the caretaker's newly polished floor and left muddy prints all over it. *But... we can solve the crime by testing the soil left behind for clues about where it came from.*

The challenge

Read the conversation on page 62 of the *Student Book* and discuss the way the students have decided to track down the soil from Mr Chopra's boots.

Relate the challenge to your own 'crime'. Produce a 'sample of soil from the polished floor' for students to examine. *How could we use what we know about different soils to catch the culprit?*

What to do

Divide the students into groups and give each group a soil sample to examine. By now they should be able to come up with several ideas on how it could yield up clues. What do they think of other students' ideas? *Have you any other ideas for testing this soil?* They might think of a soil acidity test or of adding a little water to see how sticky it becomes.

Now bring out a selection of 'teachers' shoes' and different soil samples from them. *These were removed from the possible culprits' shoes and need to be tested.*

What you need

- willing teachers with a sense of humour to be your suspects

- several shoes encrusted with different soils

- spare soil samples – try to make sure that you obtain (or manufacture) soils that are sufficiently different to show some real variation

- magnifying glasses or hand lenses

- measuring cylinders or jars

- jugs of water

- pH or 'universal' indicator strips

- sieves with different-sized holes

What to check

There are different ways of arranging this activity. Decide on whether each group has all of the samples or just one each to test. Should every group have the 'control' sample or will you use that one to demonstrate the testing techniques? Will each group do lots of different tests or just one?

Support

Make sure that the students are able to compare directly their suspect's sample with the culprit's sample. Remind them of the premise that each soil has its own 'fingerprint'.

Extend

Most students should recognize that each soil shows a different set of characteristics. Some soils may share these but by cross-referencing, the students should spot enough similarities in the sample to make a match. Which test do they think is the most and least reliable and why?

What did you find?   WS 42   WS 44

Look at the farm students' results.
Check that the students realize that to find which field Mr Chopra lost his watch in, they need to identify two identical types of soil. *Which soils have the same colour, texture, and size of particle? Do they separate in the same way?* Show that Mr Chopra's watch must be in Field 2.

Record

The students could record their data in the table provided on WS 42, then use this data to create three bar charts on WS 44.

Students can use the soil separation results to try to work out the various proportions of the different materials in the sample.

Present

Encourage the students to present their 'evidence' to solve the puzzle as a courtroom drama. Let each group contribute a piece on how they have solved the mystery. Let the students include video clips of the various stages of the investigation to make it more exciting.

Can you do better?

WS 45

Ask students how good their evidence was. How could they tackle the investigation differently if they were starting again?

Look at the farm students' investigation on WS 45 and discuss it with the students. *Would you have drawn the same conclusions? Could you have done anything better?*

Now predict

Look for an understanding that different soils are made up from different proportions of materials and that each has an individual profile that we can discover through various tests. *A single test might not give us enough information to identify a soil so we need to do several to be certain.*

Soil from the outside edges of a cultivated field may well be very different from the centre as the actions of turning, planting and digging the soils will produce a finer soil in the centre and a stonier soil at the boundaries, where it is not so heavily worked.

Sticky soil is likely to contain a high proportion of clay.

Other ideas

Soil map

Gather together the results of all your experiments and make a soil map of your area or of your school. You could eventually come up with a soil identity for each area. You may find special areas, such as cricket pitches, have a unique soil identity as they are sometimes top-dressed with marl, a mixture of clay and chalk (but please don't go digging up your local wicket!).

ICT ideas

Information from this activity could be entered into a graphing program and used to draw different types of bar and pie charts. Remind students that all graphs should have labels and that their graphs should all have titles.

At home

Remind the students that some plants grow better in certain soils than others. Ask the students to look at seed packets, plant labels and compost packaging the next time they visit a supermarket or garden centre. *What sort of information is included on the labels and what advice is given to gardeners about the best soil for each plant?*

Plenary

Play a soil identification game. Label corners of the classroom 'sand', 'clay', 'peat/humus', 'silt', 'chalk' and 'loam'. Give the students clues to identify the type of soil you are thinking of, starting with the more obscure clues and leading to obvious ones, e.g. *I started my life on a mountain, I travelled down in a stream, I'm very pale-coloured*, etc. When the students think they know the answer, they can move to stand by the correct label. Ask the students to explain their choices. Score points and give most points for the earliest correct answer.

Unit 4: Rocks and soils – Soil and water

The objectives for this lesson are that students should be able to:

- Learn that water can drain through soil

- Find out which soil drains the quickest

- Plan and take part in a scientific experiment

- Review and evaluate their evidence.

SB pp.64–65   *Starter*

- *When might water need to be filtered? Water from taps has been used several times before it finally flows into the sea. How is that possible?* Explain that the water is carefully filtered to remove all impurities. The water runs through special sand. *It's just as well it flows through quickly – or people would get very thirsty!*

- Set up an empty funnel (with a cup under it) and pour water into it. Complain that it all comes out again! Have the students any ideas about how to stop the water flowing? Use this to introduce the idea of soil as a 'water-stopper'.

The challenge

Read the conversation and What to do on page 64 of the *Student Book* and discuss Tariq's ideas. Do the students agree with him? If not, why not?

What to do

Decide together on how you are going to organize the test. *Will everyone measure the same soils? How loosely packed should your soil be? How much water should you use?* Decide whether to measure how long it takes the water to drain through to a particular depth, or the volume of water drained through in a particular time. Either choice will give you credible data. Obviously, do not attempt to measure how long all the water takes to drain through; most soils will retain some water.

What you need

- funnels or the tops of pop bottles
- rulers
- soils or components of soils – clay, sand, gravel
- a measuring jug

- a seconds timer
- cotton wool or J-cloth to prevent soil particles falling through funnels

What to check

Students should time how long it takes for an agreed amount of water (e.g. 100 ml) to flow out of each type of soil. Tell them to stop timing when the water stops dripping.

Support

Make sure that the students are measuring to the same point each time using the same units. Restrict the choice of soil material to clay, loam and sand or gravel.

Extend

Most students should recognize that the larger the particles in the soil, the faster the water drains through. Explain that this is due to the air spaces between the particles – some students may have noticed air bubbles released from the soil as the water was added. Would it make a difference if the soils were more compacted in the funnels? Why?

What did you find?   WS 46

You should find that the soil with the largest particles drains through the quickest because it is the most permeable. However, anomalous results are not unknown in this investigation! The reason a clay-type soil has poor drainage is that the particles within it are tiny. When covered in water, the surface tension of the water holds the particles tightly together, creating an impermeable layer.

Sand has more air spaces between the particles to allow the water to pass through. However, if your sand is very fine or has a chalky base, you may find that the particles bind together in the same way as clay.

Record

The students could record their data in the table provided on WS 46, then create a bar chart. The students could use Tariq's data from WS 47 if their results are inconclusive.

Present

Ask the students to make a PowerPoint presentation to 'tell the story' of the graph. *Which was the fastest draining soil? Which was the slowest?* If students have used a camera or video to make a record of their test, they could import clips into their presentations.

Can you do better?

WS 47

Ask students to review how good their evidence was. How would they tackle the investigation differently if they were starting again?

Look at the report Tariq wrote on WS 47 and discuss it with the students. Have they drawn the same conclusions? Could they have done anything better?

Now predict

Look for an understanding that permeability is only one factor we should consider when talking about soil. If a soil is too permeable then nutrients will be leached away. Farmers and gardeners add humus or other organic material to the soil to reduce the permeability and hold more water in the soil. Similarly, if a soil holds too much water (clay soil), the roots of the plants will be permanently in water and may rot away.

Packing the soil tightly will reduce the permeability by reducing the number of air spaces. This is why gardeners dig over land to be planted, to introduce air and break up compacted soil.

The best soils for growing are generally considered to be 'loams': a mixture of clay, sand and humus that holds some water but doesn't become waterlogged.

Other ideas

Make a water filter

Using different-sized particles of gravel and sand can help keep water clean. Make a filter tower using a plastic bottle filled with layers of small stones, coarse sand then fine sand. Punch holes in the bottom of the bottle and pour in muddy water. The water that flows from the bottom of the bottle is much cleaner than the water you put in. (Remember it will still contain dissolved substances and is not clean enough to drink.) This filter models how water is naturally filtered as it flows through the ground.

At home

Ask the students to try to grow fast-germinating seeds in different types of soil. Which soil is best?

Plenary

Reinforce the importance of particle size for drainage by making a living model of soil, using the students as soil particles! Arrange a group of them closely together to represent clay soil, and a second group to represent water particles. *Can the water particles find a way through?* Now ask them to pretend to be gravel soil – spaced far apart. *How many more of the water particles can push their way through now?*

New International Edition

Unit 4: Rocks and soils – Unit 4: Review

The objectives for this lesson are that students should be able to:

- Check what they have learned about rocks and soils in this Unit

- Find out how they are working within the Grade 3 level.

Expectations

Students working towards Grade 3 level will:

- Name one or two rocks

- Say that there are rocks under surfaces

- Make some measurements of time and volume.

In addition, students working within Grade 3 level will:

- Name and give characteristics of several rocks

- Explain that rocks are used for different purposes

- Recognize that there is rock under all surfaces and that soils come from rocks

- Recognize some of the properties of soil in terms of drainage

- Recognize when a test or comparison is unfair

- Measure time and volume of water carefully

- Say what their experiments and investigations show and try to explain these.

Further to this, students working beyond Grade 3 level will also:

- Explain how to make a test fair

- Explain what their experiments and investigations show in terms of the characteristics and uses of the soils and rocks tested

- Decide how good their evidence is.

Check-up

Nafisa and Yassmin could do a scratch test on their mystery rock to find out whether or not it is a diamond. As diamond will scratch every other rock, they could try to scratch another pebble on the beach. If in turn their 'diamond' became scratched, then they would know that it was something softer, such as glass.

The water remains on the impermeable base of the rock pool, but drains through the permeable sand. The sand may well be made up of similar rock, but it will have air spaces between the particles for the water to drain through.

> ⚠️ Remind students not to pick up glass.

Assessment WS 48

Use the Unit 4 assessment on WS 48 to check the students' understanding of the content of the Unit. The answers are given opposite.

Name: _____ Date: _____

WS 48 Unit 4 assessment

1 Asha's rock has a fossil of a shell in it. Sanjay's is very light and frothy and full of holes.
a) Whose rock was probably formed under the sea? Why?
_____
b) Whose rock might have come from a volcano? Why?
_____

2 Circle the name for rocks changed by temperature or pressure.
metamorphic   sedimentary   igneous

3 What are soils made from? _____

4 Oaktree School field is on sandy soil. Fernwood School field is on clay soil. One day, it rained. Which school field is likely to dry first? Why?
_____

5 What does permeable mean? _____

6 Add the names of these four soils to this branching key.
sand   clay   peat   chalk

Is the soil light coloured?
Y / N

Does it have gritty particles?
Y / N

Does it contain lots of plant remains?
Y / N

[ ]   [ ]   [ ]   [ ]

48   Heinemann Explore Science Grade 3

Answers

1 **a** Asha's, because it has fossilized shells in it, laid down in the sedimentary rock that formed in the sea millions of years ago.

 b Sanjay's, as it is pumice, which had gases trapped in it as it was bubbling up from the volcano.

2 metamorphic

3 Mainly from worn-down rocks with plant and animal material.

4 Oaktree's because their field will be the quickest to dry. Sandy soil will be better drained than clay soil.

5 Allows water to drain through.

6

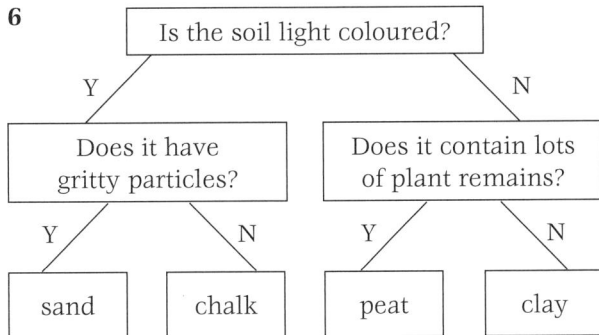

The answer!

A clay-type soil is known as a 'heavy' soil, which is mostly made of densely packed clay particles. These particles hold water in the ground and prevent surface water draining away. To make the soil less waterlogged and freer draining, Eshwar's dad would need to mix the top layer of soil with humus and sand to introduce more air spaces.

And finally...

Complete the Unit by making a rock guide of your area. Create and display a local map. Take photographs of old buildings made using interesting rocks, label them and pin the photographs on the map. Label roads, fields and gardens to show the main rock or soil features.

New International Edition

Unit 5: Magnets and springs

The objectives for this Unit are that students should be able to:

- Discover what forces are, such as magnetism

- See and learn what forces can do, even though they are invisible

- Find out how to measure forces

- Evaluate what makes a good scientific experiment.

SB p.67 | *Science background*

Without realizing that they are learning science, students can have a lot of fun with magnets and springs as they are at the heart of many toys.

It is easier to demonstrate what magnets do than to explain what one is! Magnetism is a property of iron, steel, nickel and cobalt. Some plastics have magnetic materials incorporated into them, e.g. fridge seals.

Most materials are not attracted to a magnet, but those that are can become magnetized themselves.

So how do magnets work? Magnetic metals contain clusters of particles, called 'domains', which act like individual mini-magnets. When the domains are randomly arranged, the material is not magnetic. If the domains are lined up, however, the material becomes magnetized.

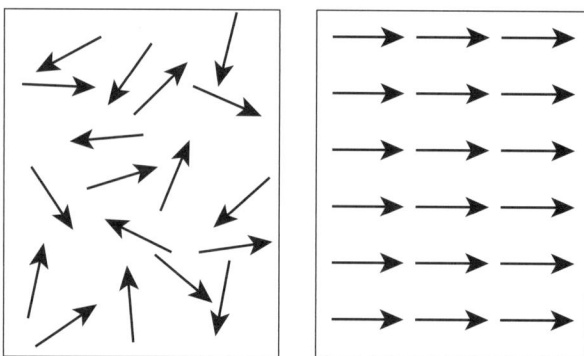

Random domains   Domains that are in line

The two ends of a magnet are called the north and south poles. Magnetism is strongest at the poles. The north pole of one magnet will attract the south of another and like poles will repel each other. Because of the north–south orientation of the magnetic domains, if a bar magnet, for example, is broken, it will still retain the north–south configuration in both halves.

Magnets act upon objects within their magnetic field. This works in three dimensions and is an invisible force within which magnetic materials will be attracted to the magnet.

Springs are found in all sorts of everyday mechanisms and are generally made of coils of metal. Springs may be difficult to spot. Did you know that your lever-arch file has a flat leaf spring in its mechanism? Energy can be stored in a spring and released later, e.g. a click-top biro pen uses a compression spring to hold it in place.

An elastic band can be used to store energy too and in this way performs like a spring. A spring will extend to what's called its 'elastic limit'. Stretched within this limit, it will return to its original shape, but stretched beyond, it will either snap or stay deformed.

Language

Pole	The ends of a magnet. The north-seeking end of a magnet points to the Earth's north magnetic pole.
Attract	To pull together.
Repel	To push or move away from.
Alloy	A mixture of two or more metals.

The Words to learn list on page 67 of the *Student Book* can be used to make a classroom display.

Resources

- *Friction and Motion* Reader.

- Selection of magnets and springs – paper springs and elastic bands are acceptable alternatives to coiled metal springs.

- Measuring tools: offer tapes, rulers, metre rules, forcemeters and measuring cylinders.

- Hoops from Physical Education classes.

- Steel paper clips.

- Balance scale or digital balance.

- Kitchen scales (operated with a spring).

- Cotton reels.

- Matchsticks.

- Beads.

Bright ideas

- Magnets get a terrible bashing in school. They quickly lose their magnetic force unless they are carefully stored with keepers. But all is not lost! Most secondary schools will be able to rejuvenate them for you, using a low-voltage coil.

- Loose iron filings are inadvisable because of the very slight danger that students might accidently rub them into their eyes. If your magnets are bearded with old filings, rub them on a doormat to brush them off. If you demonstrate with iron filings yourself, wrap the magnet in cling film – unwrapping will release the filings. You can safely use iron filings in sealed, clear plastic boxes; or you can buy them in sealed transparent 'bubbles'.

Knowledge check

Students should be able to distinguish 'metal' from other materials and be able to identify objects around them that are made of metal.

Students often believe that magnets are 'sticky' and that objects 'stick' to them. Use 'attracted to' wherever you can. As with anything invisible, a magnetic force can only be 'seen' by demonstrating what it can do!

One common misconception is that all metals must be magnetic. This is only true of nickel, cobalt, iron and steel (a mixture of iron and carbon). All other metals, including some types of stainless steel, are non-magnetic. Copper and aluminium are **not** magnetic. Some things may contain more than one type of steel, e.g. scissors may have non-magnetic stainless steel blades but a magnetic steel screw holding them together!

> ⚠ Warn students that not all metals are safe to handle – they may be sharp, rusty, or even poisonous.

Skills check

Students need to:

- make careful observations and measurements
- collect evidence and decide how good it is
- use their evidence to explain what they found out
- communicate what they have found to others.

Some students will:

- make generalizations about the nature of magnetic materials.

Links to other subjects

Literacy:	Reading and following instructions, e.g. origami frog, and comparing with other information texts. Ted Hughes's story *The Iron Man* is a good link with the subject of 'metals'.
Numeracy:	Measuring and comparing using standard units. Organizing and interpreting simple data in bar graphs and tables.
ICT:	Using a multimedia package to combine text and graphics to make a presentation.
Geography:	Using compass directions in map work.
Design and technology:	Designing and making a toy using magnets or a spring mechanism.

Let's find out...

The Unit opens with a question about spring-heeled boots.

Tell the students they are going to find out about magnets and springs so that they can answer the question.

Unit 5: Magnets and springs – Magnetic forces

The objectives for this lesson are that students should be able to:

- Learn about magnets and the forces between them

- Show that magnets exert forces without touching, by making a paper plane fly

- Find out that magnets can attract and repel each other

- Learn that magnets are used in a compass.

SB pp.68–69

Starter

- Bring in a range of other toys that use either magnets or springs in their mechanisms, e.g. magnetic board games, wind-up clockwork toys. Explain to the students that they are going to investigate the forces that make these toys work.

Explain

What is a magnet?

Discuss what students know (or think they know) about magnets and begin to introduce some of the vocabulary needed.

How does a magnet become a magnet? Demonstrate the arrangement of domains by turning the students into mini-magnets. Turn sports bibs inside out and label the front side 'N' and the back 'S' using masking tape. Dressed as magnetic particles, arrange your students randomly but closely together. Now tell them that you are a magnet and that they must always face you! As you move down them, they should end up all facing the front in straight lines. Let the students at the front and back reach out and grab things in front or behind them – they have more force, just like the poles of a real magnet.

North and south

Let students play with magnets to get the real 'feel' of the attractive and repulsive forces at work. They should discover that like poles repel and opposites attract.

Demonstrate the pattern of magnetism by putting a magnet under paper and sprinkling iron filings over it to reveal the magnetic field. Now place a damp paper towel on top of this. After a day or two, the filings will have rusted, leaving a pattern in the paper as a permanent record.

Demonstrate also that magnetic fields work in three dimensions. Suspend a magnet in a small jar of oil or syrup mixed with iron filings; the filings should group around the magnet, showing the lines of force. You can buy prepared apparatus to show this.

Very attractive

Brainstorm uses of magnets. Some, such as fridge doors, may be obvious; others, such as the magnets in doorbells, less so.

Things to do

WS 49   **WS 50**

Tug of war

When suspended and left to hang freely, a magnet orients itself to the Earth's poles. Demonstrate this by suspending a bar magnet on a string and letting it swing freely. When it comes to rest, it should always be facing the same direction. Check that this is north by using a compass.

Record

Students can compare the relative strengths of their magnets and use WS 49 to help them record the types of magnet, distance from the compass and direction of the needle.

Support

Explain that the opposite poles of the magnet attract the needle, which is why it moves. If the magnets are the same distance from the compass then the magnet the needle points to is the stronger of the two.

Extend

Ask the students what would happen if they turned the magnets round. *Do the magnets have to be placed east and west of the compass? What happens if you put them to the north and south?*

Fly a plane

Use a template from WS 50 or design your own plane to cut out and fly. If your magnets aren't strong enough to get a good result, tape two or three together with all the poles facing in the same direction.

Support

Explain that making the plane fly without the magnet touching it demonstrates that the invisible magnetic force of attraction can work through air.

Extend

How big can you make the gap between the paper clip and the magnet? Can you pass anything through the gap and still keep the plane flying? Ask them what happens if they use more than one magnet or use different paper.

Dig deeper

Find out more about magnetism and how we use magnets. Encourage more able students to make an electromagnet and explore how to magnetize metal using an electric current.

Did you know?

These facts remind students that people have known about magnetism for a very long time.

I wonder...

Look at the photograph of recycling metal on page 71 of the *Student Book*. Discuss with students why we recycle metal and how they think a magnet might help.

Other ideas

Hungry Mickey

Build your own magnetic friend. Use a painted or covered box and attach about three magnets for his mouth. Explain that Mickey is very hungry.

What would he possibly like to eat? Provide a range of magnetic and non-magnetic 'snacks' to tempt him. Only the steel and iron objects will make their way to his mouth.

Magnet maze

Students can help design and make a game that uses magnets, e.g. a maze or race track inside the top of a shoe box, with the pieces made to move using a magnet held underneath. They could include obstacles for a player to negotiate, such as humps and bridges, or stick small magnets in the box to act as traps – too close and you're caught!

Presentation

Ask the students to imagine they are television documentary makers and to prepare a presentation of the uses of magnets through the ages.

At home   WS 51

Ask the students to be a magnet detective! Where can they find magnets being used in their own homes (or in cars)? Remind them to keep safely away from electrical devices and sockets and never to put a magnet near anything electrical or close to videos, tapes, credit cards or a television screen. They can use WS 51 to help with this activity.

Plenary

Show a picture of a cow. *What possible connection could there be between cows and magnets?* Explain that farmers use powerful 'cow magnets' to protect cows from damaging themselves if they have inadvertently eaten bits of metal or barbed-wire fencing. The cows swallow the magnet and the metal is attracted to it rather than damaging the stomach lining!

Unit 5: Magnets and springs – Magnetic materials

The objectives for this lesson are that students should be able to:

- Understand how some materials are magnetic and some are not
- Plan and carry out a fair way of testing this
- Compare their results to Class 3's results
- Evaluate their own and Class 3's results.

SB pp.70–71 | Starter

- Present students with a bucket full of sawdust, paper clips, pins, bits of plastic, and any old bits and pieces. *How on Earth can I sort out this mess? I need some sawdust for a friend's hamster cage but this is all I could find and it's full of bits! It'll take forever to fish out all of the paper clips and drawing pins. Some things are sharp and might hurt the hamster. What can I do? Maybe a magnet could help? How?* Encourage the students to find out what a magnet will attract.
- Demonstrate that some metals are attracted to magnets and some aren't.

The challenge

Read the conversation on page 70 of the *Student Book* and discuss Class 3's suggestions. Ask the students to do a similar test. Were Class 3's ideas good or can they think of anything better?

What to do

Give groups of students some materials to test. Ask them to predict what will be attracted to a magnet first of all. Use PE hoops to construct a Venn diagram. Either make two separate sets or, if the students aren't sure of their predictions, they can use the central overlap as a 'not sure' category.

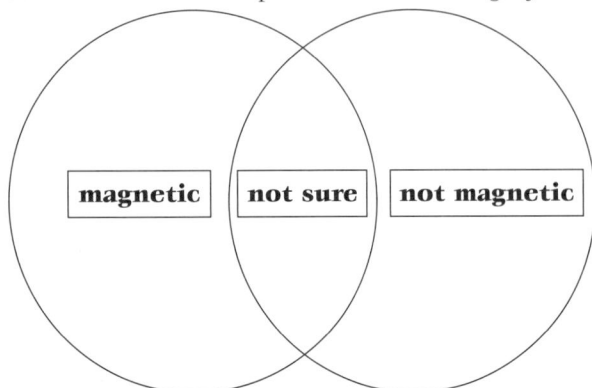

magnetic   **not sure**   **not magnetic**

What you need

- magnets
- a range of materials including both magnetic and non-magnetic metals
- PE hoops

What to check

In most cases there should be a simple 'yes' or 'no' answer to the question of whether or not something is magnetic. If you use material samples rather than real objects there should be no difficulty. If you choose to test classroom objects, however, you can have interesting results. Sometimes you might get objects made of both magnetic and non-magnetic materials, e.g. scissors with steel blades and plastic handles, or a pencil sharpener with a steel blade (magnetic) and cast zinc body (non-magnetic). It can get complicated and this is where the Venn diagram comes in useful.

Support

Reinforce what students can expect to feel when they bring a magnet close to a magnetic object. Remind students that a magnet does not have to touch the object to attract it. Students should test objects carefully to be able to feel the 'pull' of the magnetic force.

Extend

Some students may suggest that objects are made from more than one sort of metal, or that metallic metals have been plated with non-metallic ones or vice versa. For example, we often call cans 'tins', but cans are made from (magnetic) steel. The (non-magnetic) tin coating prevents corrosion. Plastic-sheathed magnets can confuse, too. It's the metal inside that's magnetic, not the plastic coat.

What did you find?   WS 52

Record

Students can use the tables on WS 52 to record their predictions and results or alternatively draw out their own Venn diagram or two-column table.

Present

Let the students compare their results with those of Class 3 on WS 53. Encourage the students to generalize from their results. They should find that only metals that contain iron are magnetic. They are unlikely to come across nickel in everyday situations and certainly not cobalt. Steel can be problematic as mentioned before – it is virtually impossible to tell one type of steel from another by sight and they may have very different properties.

A general rule might be that magnetic materials are always metals, but that not all metals are magnetic. It is worth reinforcing several times that, of the common metals students will come across, only iron and steel are magnetic. Copper, aluminium, zinc, brass, tin, gold and silver are not.

Can you do better?
WS 53

Would the students approach this investigation differently if they were asked to do it again? What would they change?

Read Class 3's report on WS 53 together. *Do you think Class 3 has drawn the right conclusions from their results? Will a stronger magnet affect the results? Will a bigger magnet be stronger?*

Now predict

Presented with two empty drink cans, are the students able to use their knowledge of magnetism to distinguish between the steel and aluminium can? Note that a very few cans have steel bodies and aluminium ends.

Other ideas

Treasure hunts

Bury pieces of magnetic metal in a sand tray and have a magnetic treasure hunt. Who can find the most pieces in the shortest time?

Extend this by burying a magnet and using the changing direction of a compass needle placed near it to find where it is buried.

ICT ideas

Use 'Alnico' as a search word on the Internet. Challenge students to find out where the name comes from. Alnico magnets (Al-ni-co) – an alloy of aluminium, nickel and cobalt – are stronger than single metal magnets.

At home
WS 54

Ask the students to use WS 54 to test magnetic materials in their homes.

Plenary

Could the students clean up the sawdust with a magnet? Can they explain why they could or could not do this? Students should be able to relate their discoveries to their understanding of magnetism, e.g. only iron and steel were attracted to the magnet. Many metals look alike, but behave differently near a magnet.

Unit 5: Magnets and springs – Strength of magnets

The objectives for this lesson are that students should be able to:

- Make predictions about which magnet will be the strongest

- Carry out an experiment to find out which is the strongest magnet

- Display their findings in a chart using ICT

- Design and make their own fridge magnets.

SB pp.72–73 — *Starter*

- *How powerful would a magnet have to be to lift and move a train? Are the most powerful magnets the biggest?*

- Show students a selection of different-sized magnets. Can they tell which is the strongest just by looking at them?

The challenge

Read the speech bubbles on page 72 in the *Student Book*. Discuss the different ways Class 3 decided to test which magnet was strongest. Why were these good – or not so good – ideas?

What to do

Split the students into groups and give each group one activity, or alternatively select only one for the whole class to complete together. However, it's a good idea to compare at least two different sets of results from different ways of testing, just to see if the strongest magnet was the strongest in both tests.

What you need

- a selection of magnets – you might like to number them for identification

- steel paper clips – preferably new ones

- a balance scale or digital balance for weighing magnets

- a water-filled measuring cylinder – it helps with retrieval to attach your magnet to a thread so it can be pulled out of the water easily

What to check

Support

Discuss how to make the test fair. Only one variable should be changed, i.e. the magnet. Everything else should be the same. Compare results from different methods later, but during each test you must keep the conditions the same.

Extend

Let the students test the strength of magnets that look identical, e.g. two bar magnets. They should realize that although they look the same, they may have differing strength. When students discover that the biggest magnet is not always the strongest, they may think that smaller magnets are always stronger, which is not the case.

What did you find?   WS 55   WS 56

To check their results, students could repeat the activity using the magnets again, or with a different set of magnets of different shapes and sizes. They should confirm that size and magnet strength are not necessarily related.

Record

If measuring the number of paper clips each magnet can pick up, students could record their data on WS 55. You could adapt this for other methods or encourage students to draw their own tables. The students could convert their recorded data into a bar chart. The data is discrete so the bars should be separate. Compare charts from each group on an acetate overlay to see if the results match. *Did everyone find that the same magnet was strongest?* If results are inconclusive, use Shameena's group's data from WS 56.

Present

Ask students to write about what they did, using a computer program if appropriate. Encourage them to compare the strengths of the various magnets.

More able students can compare the methods of testing. Encourage the use of comparative language, e.g. 'stronger', 'strongest', 'most', 'fewest', etc.

Can you do better?

Ask students to review how good their evidence was. How would they tackle the investigation differently if they were starting again?

Show the students Shameena's group's report on WS 56. Her group had predicted that bigger magnets would be stronger. Their report confirms that this idea has been disproved. It does not, however, make clear that the group realize they can't generalize that smaller magnets are always stronger. *Should we generalize that the smaller the magnet, the stronger it is? What could Shameena's group have done better?* Ask the students to criticize the report constructively.

Now predict

Discuss different magnets. Look for an understanding that strength does not depend upon size. Explain that magnets can lose their strength by being roughly treated, dropped or heated.

Other ideas

Wiped out

Your favourite music and television programmes may be stored as magnetism. Sound and video tapes are plastic ribbons with a magnetic coat. Information is recorded on the tapes as magnetic fields. Stroke them with a strong magnet and all this information and the sound and pictures will be 'wiped' and lost forever.

Let the students record their friends singing into a blank cassette tape and play it back. Then use a pencil to rewind the tape gently while rubbing a magnet over the tape as it moves. Replay the tape. *What do you sound like now?* Everything on the tape will be affected.

Hot and cold

Temperature has an effect on the strength of a magnetic force. Test the strength of a magnet and then put it in boiling water or a warm oven for 20 minutes, but take great care! (Remember not to heat a plastic-coated magnet beyond the temperature where the plastic can melt!)

Does the change in temperature affect the magnet? Extend this by freezing a magnet too; although cooling magnets often makes them stronger, they have to be really cold. Electromagnets in fusion reactors, for example, work at about −270°C.

Internet research

Using 'Maglev train' as a search term will take you into hundreds of technical sites about levitating trains, but it also offers a number of model-making ideas that might suit very able groups.

At home

Ask the students to design a fridge magnet from card or light modelling clay and attach it to a small magnet (bags of these are available from school suppliers). The weight of the design must not pull the magnet out of position.

Plenary

Present a challenge. A vital key has fallen down the back of a wooden cupboard. How can you retrieve it without moving the cupboard? Don't try this with a filing cabinet or the magnet on the string sticks to the metal!

97

Unit 5: Magnets and springs – Stretching and squeezing

The objectives for this lesson are that students should be able to:

- Discover that springs can be squashed or stretched, pushed or pulled, using force

- Learn about how and where springs are used

- Find out what happens when a spring is stretched to its limit

- Make their own springs out of a variety of materials.

SB pp.74–75 *Starter*

- Display some springs. Ask students to think of words to describe the springs such as 'bouncy', 'stretchy', 'squashy', 'strong', etc.

- Encourage students to think of other springy things, such as sponges, elastic bands and even the surfaces of some playgrounds. Offer them some springy items to stretch and squash to show how they work.

Explain

Springs

The most familiar springs are made of coiled metal, which is strong but bendy. Some springs are designed to be squashed (compression); others are made to be stretched (tension). Either way, a pushing or pulling force is needed to change the shape of a spring and the spring will push or pull back with an equal force. When the force is removed, the spring will then return to its original shape. A spring taken to its elastic limit will either break or not return to its original shape.

There are hundreds of uses for springs: sofas, beds and chairs have springs in them to push back against the weight of our bodies; so too do training shoes. Remember any springy material such as sponge or rubber can act like a spring. We use springs for fun as in a pinball machine, on a trampoline or on a pogo stick. Many springs work with catches, e.g. biro pens, umbrellas and your computer's CD-ROM tray.

Watch out!

The hairspring in a watch is a different style of spring – a flat coil. There are also flat 'leaf' springs, made up of a sandwich of metal, on some trailers and lorries. A leaf spring opens a stapler.

That's the limit

Discuss what happens when you keep stretching a spring or an elastic band. Illustrate this by stretching a springy balloon, showing the students that it returns to its original size after it's been stretched. Now blow it up and continue until it pops. (Protect your eyes.) You've just demonstrated the elastic limit of a balloon.

Things to do WS 57 WS 58

Measure a force

Reinforce the fact that springs can be stretched or squashed and that the force of the stretch or squash can be measured. Sometimes measuring this force can be useful to us. Bring in kitchen scales that operate with a spring (rather than a suspended balance) and let the students feel how much force they need to use to move the pointer.

Make a forcemeter, using the instructions on WS 57.

Record

Let very able students record the correlation between mass (gm) and force (N) and plot the information on a line graph.

Support

Ask students to hold a 1 kg mass in their hand. They should feel the heavy mass pushing down on their hand as the mass is pulled by gravity towards the floor. Put a 100 g mass in their other hand. Does it feel the same? We can measure this force by attaching the masses to an elastic band. Which mass do the students think will stretch the band the most?

Extend

The 100 g mass exerts a force of 1N. Ask the students to estimate the amount of pull exerted on their forcemeter by objects around the classroom.

Paper frog

Instructions for making an origami frog are given on WS 58.

You may need to demonstrate each step in the process of folding the paper. Use an enlarged sheet of paper with colour on one side only to demonstrate each fold; stiff wrapping paper works well.

Did you know?

Remind students that springs and all things springy have an elastic limit including a bungee!

I wonder...

Hard things are springy too. Even a solid object such as a marble will deform slightly when it hits a hard floor, squashing minutely and then springing back into shape as it bounces. The speed with which something gets back its shape determines how well it bounces. 'Superballs' are made to regain their shape very quickly, and so they bounce very high.

Other ideas

Pop-ups

Make a pop-up card using different types of spring. Students could use paper or card folded in a zigzag, two strips folded over and over each other in a concertina or a wire wound round a pencil.

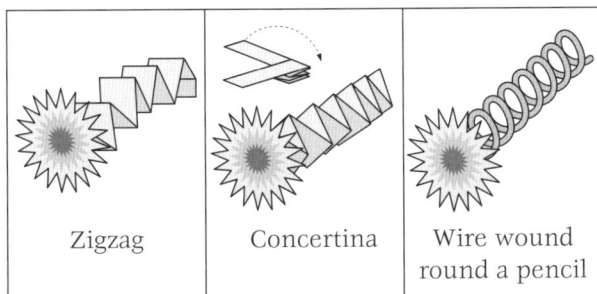

| Zigzag | Concertina | Wire wound round a pencil |

Death-defying doll

Collect an assortment of children's dolls and have a bungee competition using thick elastic bands or, better still, ribbon elastic as bungees. If the dolls have different masses, the students will need to compensate for this by lengthening or shortening the elastic; the heavier dolls will stretch the elastic more. Remind the students that the object of this game is not for the doll to be smashed on the ground!

Presentation

Ask the students to imagine that they are opening a bric-a-brac shop specializing in collections of everyday objects that contain springs. Invite them to bring in items from home, as well as using those found in the classroom, and ask them to label each one. Can they say where the springs can be found?

At home

The students probably won't need much encouragement to measure the elasticity of some sweets! *When you stretch them, do they go back to their original length? How far can you stretch them before they snap or get eaten?* Jelly-type sweets are usually less elastic than rubber or elastic bands so you can expect them to remain slightly longer after stretching and not exactly go back to their original length.

Plenary

Ask students to examine an everyday object such as a stapler, a paper punch or a retractable pen and to explain where the springs are, what type of springs they are and what their function is. *How would the tool work without a spring?*

Unit 5: Magnets and springs – Exploring springs

The objectives for this lesson are that students should be able to:

- Make paper springs to test their strength

- Explore how far their springs can stretch

- Take accurate measurements of their results

- Evaluate their results, looking for a pattern.

SB pp.76–77

Starter

- It's classroom challenge time! Sitting where they are, how many springy things can the students spot? Is there a door closer, a window catch, a window blind, a stretchy cable to the computer? There are springs in the fabrics that they are wearing and even their body joints. *We need springs. Some springs are strong and some are weak.* The students are going to investigate a really weak spring!

The challenge

Read the conversation on page 76 of your *Student Book* and Class 3's ideas. Explain to the students that you're using paper rather than elastic or wire springs because you'll be testing the spring to its elastic limit. Tested beyond its elastic limit, wire or elastic might snap back and hurt somebody, whereas paper will only tear.

What to do

Secure the centre of the spring to the back of a chair placed on top of a table to ensure a big drop. Let the spring hang down and secure a paper clip to the free end. Now you are ready to measure.

What you need

- a paper spiral

- scissors

- sticky tape

- paper clips

- metre rulers or tapes

- graph paper

What to check

WS 59

As there is a lot of measuring involved in this activity, ensure that students understand which distances they are measuring. There are a couple of choices: the distance the spring has stretched from the top of the chair to the bottom of the spiral, and the distance from the floor to the bottom of the spring. Either way, the students should get a measurement of the gradually extending spring. Often students get carried away and turn measuring sticks upside down without realizing it. This is a good opportunity to consolidate their knowledge of measures; make sure they measure from the same point each time. Students can then record their results on WS 59.

Support

Cutting a spiral can be tricky. Draw a master onto paper and photocopy it for students to follow. Bear in mind that cuts or tears in the spiral may weaken the spring so you need to make the spiral thick enough to withstand any unevenness.

Extend

Compare the results of the paper spring with those using the same spiral made of card or tissue. Crêpe paper, although difficult to cut, provides interesting results as it is very stretchy itself.

Some students might realize that the spring does not stretch equally with each added paper clip and that at some point the spring stops stretching even though they are adding more clips.

What did you find?

WS 60

Record

The students can use WS 60 to record their results. This data is continuous so it should be recorded on a line graph. Alternatively, bridge the gap between this and a bar chart by making a stick graph instead. If the students' results are inconclusive, they could use the data for Class 3's results in the *Student Book*.

Present

Ask the students to try to explain the graph. It is important to notice that the spring does not extend evenly and eventually stops.

Ask students to present their findings in groups – particularly useful if you have made springs from different types of paper. If students have taken photographs of their experiment, they could incorporate these into a PowerPoint presentation. They should also include their tables and graphs.

Can you do better?
WS 61

Ask students how good their evidence was. How could they tackle the investigation differently if they were starting again?

Class 3's teacher asked for the results to be averaged to make them more reliable. Read Class 3's report on WS 61 together. *Do you think Class 3 has drawn the right conclusion from the results? How do your results compare with Class 3's?*

Stretching a paper spring, releasing and stretching it again can give variable results.

Now predict

Cutting the paper spring in different thicknesses will change its properties. The thinner the spring, the more it will stretch. Thicker springs take more weight to change their shape. Students can predict the thickness of springs in watches, in lorries and in a pogo stick. *How are springs matched to the task?*

Other ideas

Hot and cold

Use thin elastic bands for this experiment. Attach a yoghurt pot to a thin elastic band and hook the elastic over a pencil or rail so that it hangs down. Measure the length of the band then add small weights (marbles or beans) to the pot. Measure the band after each weight is added. Keep adding but be careful – when the band breaks you don't want the weights falling on your feet or a yoghurt pot in the eye. Make a graph of your results. What happens just before the band breaks?

Now repeat the experiment with a band that has been in a freezer and one that you have warmed up with a hairdryer. *Does the temperature affect the breaking point?*

Graphing

Information from the yoghurt pot activity can be entered into the graphing program and used to draw a range of graphs. Remind the students that the independent variable (the number of paper clips) should be on the x-axis and that the dependent variable (length of stretched spring) needs to be on the y-axis. Agree on a descriptive title for the graphs.

At home
WS 59

Let the students take their spirals home to use creatively as hanging mobiles. Suggest that they decorate them as monkeys' tails or snakes and use paper clips to extend them to different heights.

They can try the activity again at home using WS 59 to help them.

Plenary

Ask students to begin to generalize, using an 'e-r, e-r' statement. For example, 'the thinn**er** the spring, the great**er** the stretch' or 'the heav**ier** the weight, the long**er** the stretch'. Generalizations like these will help them to see beyond their individual results and to put their ideas in a more general context.

Unit 5: Magnets and springs – Spring power

The objectives for this lesson are that students should be able to:

- Learn about elasticity by testing elastic bands
- Find out which is the springiest elastic band
- Plan how they can make their experiment a fair test
- Present their 'tank Olympics' using ICT.

SB pp.78–79

Starter

- Explain that elastic bands are very useful because they're springy. When we pull an elastic band, the force we use makes it change shape. We can feel it pulling back on our hand. If we stop pulling and let go, the elastic will return to its original shape. We call this ability to return to its original size and shape 'elasticity'.

- Some modern plastics have elastic properties. You may have spectacle frames that you can demonstrate being bent, sat on and generally pulled about, yet still return to their original shape, almost as if they 'remember' it.

The challenge

Show the students a model of the tank they're going to make. Explain that it works because the elastic stores energy in it as you wind it. When you release the elastic, it will return to its original shape and release all of the stored energy. By attaching the stick, you can change this stored energy into movement.

What to do

To begin with, it is simpler to have each group follow the instructions and construct the same model. You may find you need to adjust the length of the match or the position of the pencil to make the tank run straight.

What you need

- a selection of elastic bands
- cotton reels (plastic ones are available from science suppliers)
- short pencils
- spent matchsticks or craft matchsticks
- beads with holes large enough for the elastic to be pushed through
- rulers
- sticky tape

If you don't have cotton reels, any cylindrical object will do, e.g. drink cans, plastic bottles or film canisters. For these, however, you will need to take care when punching holes in the ends. Drink cans work very well but you may have to wrap thick elastic bands around the body of the tank to increase friction with the surface as they tend to skid around a bit.

What to check

Encourage students to answer in terms of 'force'.

Support

Counting is important in this activity so be certain that students are able to do this confidently. Be prepared to support less dextrous students in the 'making' stage so that they don't become frustrated.

Extend

Most students should recognize that the more winds they give to the elastic band, the further the tank will travel. Some might notice that the tank gets slower as the elastic unwinds. Students could use a seconds timer to time each run. Do the most winds produce the fastest tanks?

What did you find?   WS 62   WS 63

There will be a general rule unique to each tank. For example, 'Our tank travelled 8 cm for each turn of the pencil'.

Record

The students could record their data on WS 62 then convert this data into graphs. The number of winds should be entered on the x-axis and the distance travelled on the y-axis.

Alternatively, record the results of using different elastic bands as a bar chart, showing type of band on the x-axis and distance travelled through a number of turns on the y-axis. If the students' data is inconclusive, they could use Class 3's data on WS 63.

Present

Construct a 'tank Olympics' with a racetrack and events for different categories of vehicle. Have a winners' podium for gold, silver and bronze winners in different events, e.g. longest distance travelled with 30 winds, straightest line, fastest over 1 m.

The students could use a video camera to record the race and add a sports-event-style commentary, paying particular attention to the features that made each tank a 'winner'. They could incorporate their graphs and tables into a presentation using a PowerPoint template.

Can you do better?

Ask students how good their evidence was. How could they tackle the investigation differently if they were starting again?

Look at the report Class 3 wrote on WS 63 and discuss it with the students. *Have you drawn the same conclusions as Class 3? Could Class 3 have done anything better?*

Now predict

Look for an understanding that the energy put into the spring/elastic relates directly to the energy released. They have converted the potential (stored) energy of the elastic into movement but they can't get more energy out than they put in. Students should predict that the more winds, the further the tank will travel.

Note differences due to the thickness of the elastic. Thin bands will store less energy than thicker ones, although they may be easier to wind. You get out of a spring what you put into it!

Other ideas

Catapulting cars

A simple way to demonstrate the 'pushing power' of elastic is to make a catapult to propel a toy car along a flat surface by fixing elastic between two poles or the legs of a chair. Students should predict how far the car will travel if the elastic is stretched by different amounts.

At home

WS 64

Invite the students to make a similar experiment on water rather than on land. Use the diagram on WS 64 as a template to make an elastic-powered boat. Let the students take their boat home and test it in the bath!

Plenary

Using a digital camera or video camera, students can prepare an information presentation on 'How to make a tank'. Suggest that it includes design tips and ideas on how to improve the tank that are based on their discoveries. Encourage them to explain their discoveries in terms of force rather than just observations.

Unit 5: Magnets and springs – Unit 5: Review

The objectives for this lesson are that students should be able to:

- Check what they have learned about magnets and springs in this Unit

- Find out how they are working within the Grade 3 level.

Students working towards Grade 3 level will:

- Describe what happens when some materials are put near a magnet

- With help, test an idea and make a comparison between results.

In addition, students working within Grade 3 level will:

- Recognize that a force acts in a particular direction

- Describe the direction of forces between magnets or between a spring and someone compressing it

- Classify materials as magnetic or non-magnetic and describe some uses of magnets

- Suggest how to test an idea, explaining how to make a simple test fair

- Draw conclusions from results and suggest reasons for these

- Communicate what they have found out with others

- Measure simple forces.

Further to this, students working beyond Grade 3 level will also:

- Describe the difference between a magnet and a magnetic material

- Explain results in terms of their scientific knowledge and understanding.

Check-up

Discuss the situation with the students. They should be able to tell you that, all other things being equal, the thick band will send the ball further. It is harder to pull the thick elastic band; it requires more force than the thin band to move it the same distance, so when the elastic is released, the ball will be released with more force from the thick elastic than from the thin band.

Check that the force of magnetic repulsion is making the toy move.

Assessment   WS 65

Use the Unit 5 assessment on WS 65 to check students' understanding of the Unit. The answers are given opposite.

Name: _____   Date: _____

WS 65

Unit 5 assessment

1 What will happen when these magnets are brought together?
   a) [S][N] [N][S] _____
   b) [S][N] [S][N] _____

2 Samra is testing materials with a magnet. Underline the things that are attracted to her magnet.
   aluminium foil   steel can   plastic comb
   copper wire   wooden ruler   iron nail

3 Michael has a Jack-in-the-box toy. It works with a spring. Draw what you think the spring looks like when the box is closed.

   Explain what happens when Michael opens the box.

4 Class 3 are investigating paper springs. They add paper clips to their spring, one at a time, and draw a graph of their results. Which graph do the students draw? _____
   a) Length of stretch / Number of clips
   b) Length of stretch / Number of clips
   c) Length of stretch / Number of clips

   Explain why you chose this graph. _____

Unit 5: Magnets and springs   65

Answers

1   **a**   They will repel each other (push away).

     b   They will attract each other.

2   steel can, iron nail

3   Any indication of a compressed spring.

    Accept the spring will bounce upwards, the energy will be released, the spring will go back to its original shape, the spring will push up.

4   Students should choose a) – the one graph that indicates the gradual slowing of the extension of the spring as it reaches the elastic limit.

    They should explain that the spring does not extend regularly and the intervals will reduce as the spring extends to its elastic limit. Accept any indication that the graph shows a more gentle curve towards the end and that eventually the spring will not stretch any more.

The answer!

Discuss how the students now know that springs will only return the force put into them. Maybe a very powerful electromagnet would have been able to lift them but then they'd need to be wearing an iron coat and have an accomplice to switch the magnet off and let them down!

And finally…

Complete the Unit by displaying a range of toys and everyday objects that use magnets and springs in their mechanisms. Set up the range of interactive activities alongside the students' enquiry results, graphs and conclusions. Use your ceiling space to dangle paper springs and key questions.

New International Edition

Unit 6: Friction

The objectives for this Unit are that students should be able to:

- Understand that friction is a force that slows things down

- Learn that forces can be measured and that friction is measured in newtons (N)

- Make careful observations and measurements for a fair test

- Develop their scientific investigation and evaluation skills.

SB p.81   *Science background*

Friction is a force that can be a help or a hindrance to us. It acts between moving surfaces to slow the movement down and changes the moving or kinetic energy into heat. Friction can happen between any surfaces – they do not need to feel rough, they could feel smooth. Most friction results because surfaces rubbing together are not completely smooth. At a microscopic level, you can see hills and valleys on the surfaces that bump together and slow down movement.

There is another factor in friction called molecular attraction. This causes extremely smooth surfaces to stick to each other due to molecular forces, e.g. cling film sticks to plates and bowls.

Friction doesn't only exist between solid surfaces. Objects moving through air or water that present a large surface area create more friction than do more narrow, streamlined shapes.

Language

Friction	A force acting against a moving object, making it slow down or stop.
Air resistance	The force of friction acting on moving objects in air.
Water resistance	The force of friction acting on moving objects in water.
Forcemeter	A device for measuring forces in newtons (N).
Newton	The unit of measurement of forces (N).
Surface area	The outside of something. The bigger the outside, the bigger the surface area.
Lubricant	Anything used to reduce friction when two surfaces rub together, e.g. water or oil.
Streamlining	Making an object long, smooth and narrow to reduce air or water resistance.

The Words to learn list on page 81 of the *Student Book* can be used to make a classroom display.

Resources

- *Friction and Motion* Reader.

- Range of forcemeters.

- Range of surfaces, e.g. card, paper, carpet, sandpaper, felt, cork, vinyl, etc.

- A ramp.

- Toy cars.

- Measuring tools – offer tapes, rulers, metre rules.

- Digital camera.

- Seconds timer (capable of measuring to 0.1 seconds).

- Wooden blocks.

- Pop bottles or sweet jars.

- Wallpaper paste.

- Plasticine.

- Marbles.

- Lubricants, e.g. water, oil, liquid soap.

Bright ideas

- Sports centres and DIY shops are good sources for off-cuts of 'surfaces' for many of the experiments. They may also have ceramic or cork floor tiles they can let you have. If there is a garden centre attached, you may even be able to acquire some real turf!

- Your friendly sports centre manager may be able to provide you with a left-over metre or two of AstroTurf, which is an excellent surface for testing friction. Old rubber and vinyl gym mats or vaulting spring surfaces are also very useful.

Knowledge check

- Students should identify friction as a force. Friction is a force that opposes movement; there can be friction between solid surfaces and other solids, liquids and gases. They should describe some of the factors that increase friction between solid surfaces.

- Students should know how to measure a force and that gravity is a force that pulls everything towards the centre of the Earth. Students often think of forces in terms of movement. One misconception that students often hold is that if an object isn't moving, then there are no forces acting on it.

- It is a common belief that heavy objects sink and light objects float. Whether an object floats or sinks (in air or in water) depends upon its volume in relation to its mass, the material it's made from and the density of the gas or liquid it's in.

Skills check

Students need to:

- make careful observations and measurements

- collect evidence and decide how good it is

- use their evidence to explain what they found out

- be able to describe situations in which frictional forces are helpful as well as those in which frictional forces resist motion.

Links to other subjects

Literacy: Reading and following instructions. *Flat Stanley* by Jeff Brown is a humorous starting point for any work on kites. Read *The Mighty Slide* poem by Allan Ahlberg about making a playground ice slide.

Numeracy: Measuring and comparing using standard units. Organizing and interpreting simple data in bar graphs and tables. Decimal numbers. Measuring time to 0.1 seconds.

ICT: Using multimedia packages to combine text and graphics to make a presentation. Using spreadsheets to record and analyse data. Using a light sensor.

Geography: Investigating weather, recording of wind and the Beaufort scale.

Art: Using different surfaces and materials to make a collage. Picasso's pictures of violins are good to copy using newspaper, brown paper and corrugated cardboard. Violins make a sound because of friction between bow and strings.

Design and technology: Investigating how wind and water power are harnessed by windmills, wind farms, dams, waterwheels, sails and boats. Building a kite, glider, windsock or boat.

Let's find out

The Unit opens with this question:

> Haniya's grandad slipped on his bathroom floor tiles. He wasn't hurt but he wanted his home to be made safer for him. Haniya and her mum are changing things in the bathroom and kitchen so that nothing will be too slippery. What changes could they make?

Discuss the problem with the students and encourage them to suggest solutions. Open up the discussion to include reasons why some things are slippery and others are not. Think about the surfaces of playground slides as opposed to the surface of the playground itself. *What happens to these surfaces when it rains?* Elicit that smooth, wet surfaces are more slippery than dry, rough ones. (But note that students will stick to wet playground slides!) Tell the students they are going to find out about different surfaces and how objects move on or through them.

107

Unit 6: Friction – What is friction?

The objectives for this lesson are that students should be able to:

- Observe how friction slows things down and can make moving things stop

- Find out how and why lubrication reduces friction between objects

- Discover how friction produces heat

- Research where friction can be useful or a nuisance.

SB pp.82–83

Starter

- Show a picture of children sliding on ice. *Imagine children were playing outside on a cold day. Where would they find some slippery surfaces? What do some countries do to stop vehicles slipping on the roads or to stop people slipping on icy pavements?*

Explain

Get a grip

Friction is a force that is acting on us all the time. It happens when two surfaces rub together and grip. This gripping happens at a molecular level. Friction opposes movement; in other words, it slows things down and eventually it can make moving objects stop.

How friction works

Most of the time we can tell whether a surface is smooth or rough. At a microscopic level, however, no surface is absolutely smooth. The interaction between the microscopic hills and valleys between one surface and another gradually slows down movement between them. Use a model made out of interlocking bricks to represent a highly magnified surface. Make a crenellated pattern of bricks and try moving them over each other. You'll soon find that they stick! This is an extreme example of friction. If you put a piece of paper between the two brick layers, you'll find you can move them very easily – you've just lubricated the surface!

This also shows that often two very similar surfaces grip with a lot of force, even though they may appear to have very smooth surfaces (think of trying to rub two sheets of cling film across each other).

Slipping and sliding

Different surfaces have different amounts of friction. The most important aspects of friction that students encounter are in slowing things down and stopping slipping. Talk about the treads on shoes or tyres.

Remember that the larger the surface area of the tread in contact with the ground, the greater the friction. Generally, the rougher the surface, the more friction there is.

Skate away

Ice, particularly wet ice, has very little friction. The relationship between force, pressure and friction is complex and, in the context of winter sports, it is sufficient to explain that reducing surface area will reduce friction. Note, however, that ice-skating is different. The ice actually melts under the blade of the skate and so the skater is floating on a film of water. The ice freezes again almost immediately.

Things to do   WS 66

Friction and heat

The friction between the palms of our hands produces heat. Lubrication, such as water, can reduce friction and so reduce heat. The palms of our hands are two similar and relatively smooth surfaces; rubbing them together causes the ridges on the similar surfaces to collide and produce friction.

Record

Make a collection of fingerprints showing the different patterns of ridges and troughs. Let the students press their finger onto clear sticky tape, mount them in a slide case, then project the prints through a slide projector onto a screen.

Support

Use a hand magnifier to show students the ridges and troughs on the palms of their hands in more detail.

Extend

Students could investigate other lubricants such as cooking oil, baby oil, liquid soap, hand lotion or talcum powder and see which reduces the friction between their palms the most effectively.

Marbles

To make this race even more challenging, let the students use chopsticks or two pencils to lift the marbles. Adding oil lubricates the surface and should make the marbles more difficult to grip.

Record

Bicycles are great for investigating high and low friction. Students can use WS 66 to label all the examples of friction you can find, e.g. brake blocks, tyre tread, handlebar grips, etc.

Support

Let the students dip their hands in a bowl of light cooking oil and encourage them to rub their hands together to feel the slipperiness of oil (messy but effective).

Extend

Outside, make a slide from a length of guttering raised at an angle. With a stopwatch, let the students time how long it takes a toy figure to reach the bottom of the dry slide. Then train a hosepipe on the slide to create a flume. Ask them to time the toy figure's descent now. This time, the water is acting as a lubricant so the journey should be faster.

Exploring

Students should research 'friction and lubrication' using the Internet for more information. Students can also find out how to reduce friction.

Did you know?

The facts illustrate that friction can be useful as well as a force that needs to be overcome.

I wonder...

Bike brakes work by the frictional effect of a rubber brake block tightly gripping the wheel rim. Although both surfaces are smooth, there is a high frictional force between them, which slows the bike down. On a wet day, the water will get between these surfaces and act as a lubricant, reducing friction and making the brakes less effective.

Other ideas

Twist off

Collect some empty jars and bottles with differently sized or shaped screw-top lids. Tighten the lids. Ask the students, without letting them touch the jars, which lid will be the hardest and easiest to get off. Try it. Were they correct?

Presentation

Ask students to use word-processing and drawing software to describe all of the sources of friction they can think of and how these might be a help or a hindrance to us.

At home

Ask the students to make an inventory of friction and lubrication and how they are used in their home.

Plenary

The movie *Cool Runnings* is about the first Jamaican bobsled team and their move from downhill kart racing on grass and tarmac to Olympic stardom on ice. Select clips from the movie to share and discuss with the students to revisit what they have learned so far.

Unit 6: Friction – Measuring forces

The objectives for this lesson are that students should be able to:

- Explore the forces needed to move an object across a surface
- Plan and carry out a scientific investigation to measure force
- Learn how to measure and record force in newtons
- Present their findings using ICT.

SB pp.84–85 — Starter

- Remind the students of how we measure forces using a spring that stretches inside a device called a forcemeter or newtonmeter.
- Tell the students that they are going to investigate the amount of force needed to drag objects over a surface.

The challenge

Read the start of page 84 of the *Student Book* and discuss Haniya's ideas. Ask the students to do a similar test. *Are Haniya's ideas good or can you think of anything better?*

What to do

Let the students carry out the investigation in groups. Ask them to predict how much force will be needed to start the dish moving. *Would your prediction change if you added marbles to the dish?* Discuss the reasons behind the students' answers.

What you need

- a small plastic dish
- string
- a forcemeter or newtonmeter
- marbles or small masses (e.g. coins)

What to check

Students will have to pull very slowly and carefully to gauge the exact moment that the dish moves. Encourage the students to increase their pulling force gradually, taking up the strain first of all as in a tug of war. Tugging or pulling with too much force will give inaccurate readings. It's probably best to do this with one student pulling, one spotting the

movement and one with an eye on the forcemeter to note the measurement. Alternatively, you could set up a computer motion sensor or light gate to sense when the dish has moved.

Support

Reinforce the fact that all conditions apart from the number of marbles should be the same. If, for example, the students change the shape of the dish or the material it's made from, they will get a different result.

Extend

All students should be able to distinguish that some force is needed to start the dish moving and that a dish full of marbles needs a greater force to move it than an empty dish. Some students will be able to recognize a pattern between the number of marbles in the dish and the increased force needed to move them. They should begin to draw conclusions, linking the mass of the object to the force needed to move it.

What did you find? — WS 67

Record

Students can use the table on WS 67 to record their results or alternatively draw out their own table. The students should plot their results on a line graph, with the mass or number of marbles on the x-axis and the force needed to move them on the y-axis. As a fallback, they could use Haniya's results in the *Student Book*. Their results should form a regular, straight (or nearly straight) line, indicating a direct relationship between the two variables. Let them use the graph to predict the force needed to move other values on the x-axis that they haven't tried yet. Were their predictions correct?

Present

Encourage the students to generalize from their results and make a presentation from them. They should find that the bigger the reading on the forcemeter, the more difficult it is to get an object moving. The general rule could be that the heavier the object is, the more difficult it is to move or the more force is needed to start to move it. This is an important point for students to remember when they complete other friction experiments, such as using friction ramps to see which shoe has the most slippery sole, as students may forget to keep the mass of the shoes constant.

Can you do better?

WS 68

Show the students the report on WS 68. Read it together. *Has Haniya kept the investigation fair? What could she have improved? What did Haniya do differently to you?*

Would the students approach this investigation differently if they were asked to do it again? Were there factors they should have controlled better?

Friction investigations often surprise, and students are tempted to rig their results.

Now predict

Both the surface area of the container and the actual surface it is dragged across will have an effect on the results of this investigation. Generally, if two objects have the same mass and surface but different surface areas, the object with the largest area in contact with the table top will have more friction and will be more difficult (need more force) to move. However, with the kinds of surface areas and masses you are likely to be using in school, these differences will not be dramatic. On the other hand, using a very rough surface and contrasting the results with a highly polished surface should give demonstrably different results.

As Haniya removes objects from the dish, the dish becomes lighter; less force is needed to start it moving and so it should be easier to move.

Other ideas

Weights on wheels

Wheels reduce friction and make moving things easier. If you put a heavy object on wheels, you are effectively reducing the surface area in contact with the ground and so reducing the frictional forces at work. As the wheel turns, only a very small part of its surface is in contact with the ground at any time.

Demonstrate this effect using pencils. Instead of dragging the marble-filled dish across a level surface, try putting pencils under it to act as rollers. You should find the dish much easier to move!

ICT ideas

If you have one, you could use a motion sensor or light gate to monitor when your objects move. Record the results from your investigations on a spreadsheet and use the information to construct bar charts and graphs.

At home

WS 69

Ask the students to make a list of heavy objects around the home that have been mounted on wheels, e.g. television, computer table, some lounge chairs, etc. *Why is it important that some objects, although they are extremely heavy such as washing machines, do not have a full set of wheels?*

Ask students to complete WS 69.

Plenary

Revisit the idea that the heavier an object is, the more force will be needed to move it across a surface. Explain the method of using rollers (or wheels) to move heavy objects. Tell the students that some scientists and historians believe that a similar method was used in ancient times to move the large stones used to build monuments such as Stonehenge in the UK. The Ancient Egyptians, who built the pyramids, were thought to have used sledges. Challenge the students to find large masses that they can safely move in this way.

Unit 6: Friction – Slippery surfaces

The objectives for this lesson are that students should be able to:

- Find out which surface is the most slippery

- Compare the test results for two or more moving objects

- Explain their findings and display them in a bar chart

- Evaluate the good points of their investigation.

SB pp.86–87

Starter

- Display a picture of Sir Isaac Newton. *Who can tell me anything about Isaac Newton?* Establish that he was a scientist who first explained the force of gravity. Challenge the students by saying that Isaac Newton was wrong! You have discovered a way to defy gravity and you can control whether something falls to the ground or not.

- For this trick, you will need aluminium foil, a pen or pencil and some string. Scrunch the foil into a loose ball and use the pen to poke a hole halfway through the ball at an angle. Then poke another hole through the ball from the other side, again at an angle, so the two holes meet, creating a 'V' shape inside the ball. Next, push the string through the hole. When you hold the string vertical and loose the ball should slowly slide down the string. When you tighten the string, the ball should stop moving as the friction between the string and the foil ball will be sufficient to stop the ball's gravity.

- Now invite the students to think about how the trick works! Tell them that the clue is all to do with friction and that this lesson is all about friction between solid surfaces.

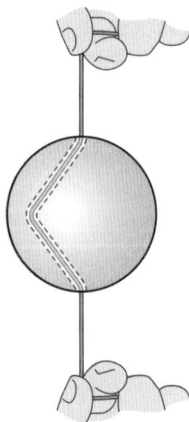

The challenge

Read the conversation on page 86 in the *Student Book* and discuss the ideas with the students. *How good do you think they are? Why did the students think they should look at the racing surface first?* What effect do the students anticipate this will have? Can the students predict the effects of changing any of the other variables mentioned such as weight or size of tyres?

What to do

Discuss how to tackle this investigation and what equipment you might need. There are many variables that could be changed in an investigation like this so be sure that the students know exactly what they are testing and what they are measuring.

Are you all going to do the same thing? Split the students into groups. Mr Khan's class chose to test the surface of the ramp so that is what they changed – everything else was kept the same. (Ideally, students should have at least three of their own results to compare.)

What you need

- a wooden block or similar to act as your 'vehicle'

- a ramp or plank – PE benches work well for races because they are long. You may have to build up the edges with card to stop objects slipping off the sides.

> ⚠ When raising the benches up, be careful to secure them as they could cause injury if they fell on someone's feet. Take care with raising any ramp up on bricks – too high and it could fall.

- materials to cover the surface. Interesting materials include felt, tissue paper, corrugated card, rubber and bubble wrap.

- a metre ruler

- books or bricks to support the end of your plank

What to check

The students need to decide what they are going to measure. They could measure the height the ramp needed to be before the block started to move on each surface.

Support

Discuss how to make the test fair. To make measuring easier, use non-standard, easily 'countable' units such as books.

Heinemann Explore Science

Extend

More able students may enjoy the challenge of measuring the angle of incline rather than the height of the ramp. Encourage them to design an angle measurer to help in their recording.

What did you find?   WS 70

Record

The students can use the table provided on WS 70 to record their results.

The students could convert their recorded data into a bar chart. The data is discrete so a bar chart is more appropriate than a line graph.

Present

Encourage them to look at their graph and 'tell its story'. Ask the students to present their findings in groups. *Which material was the stickiest? Which was the most slippery?*

Encourage the use of comparative language, e.g. higher, highest, lower, lowest, more slippery, most slippery.

Can you do better?

Ask the students to review how good their evidence was. How would they tackle the investigation differently if they were starting again?

Show the students the data from Mr Khan's class in the *Student Book. How can we generalize about changing the surface of the ramp? What could the class have done better?* Ask the students to criticize the report constructively.

Students may also have noticed that even though sandpaper is very rough, it is relatively slippery. Explain this apparently anomalous result by looking at sandpaper through a magnifying lens. Its surface is covered in sharp peaks; only the tips of these peaks are in contact with the wooden block, not the entire surface of the sandpaper. This reduced surface area reduces the amount of friction.

Lubricating the ramps may well reduce the friction – particularly on the smoother surfaces. However, we cannot recommend pouring baby oil over felt or carpet!

Now predict

Discuss the different possibilities. The students should show an understanding that the slipperiness of a surface depends upon the interaction of two surfaces, e.g. two surfaces which create friction between them even if, individually, they feel smooth.

Other ideas

Slippery shoes

Ask the students to look at the soles of their friends' shoes. *Which shoe do you think would be the most slippery and why?* Let them make press prints of the soles on squared paper and calculate the surface area. Display the footprints around the classroom.

ICT ideas

Students can use a spreadsheet to record the height of the different surfaces before the block started to move. They can then sort the materials in order and construct a bar chart of their results.

At home   WS 71

Ask the students to shove a coin across various surfaces and measure how far it travels. They could try on a wooden table, then on a polished table. *On which surface does your coin travel further? Why?*

Ask students to complete WS 71.

Plenary

Remind students of the predictions they made before they started their enquiry. Were they correct?

Remember the hanging ball trick? Explain to the students how the trick worked. The friction between the string and the sides of the channel through the ball stopped its descent when the string was pulled tight against the sides. When you relax the tension and the string is no longer held against the side, the ball slips down.

113

Unit 6: Friction – Different forces

The objectives for this lesson are that students should be able to:

- Discover that friction exists in liquids and gases, such as air
- Observe how air and water friction slow things down
- Find out what a streamlined shape is
- Research Admiral Beaufort and his wind scale.

SB pp.88–89   *Starter*

- Display a picture of a kite. Explain that the students are going to find out all about how things move in air.

The challenge

Forces all around

A dramatic way to show students the force of the surrounding air is to use air pressure to crush a plastic bottle! Take a 2-litre plastic pop bottle and put a cup of very hot water in it. Swirl the water around for a minute or two to warm the bottle and the air inside it. Secure the bottle top and plunge the bottle into a bowl of ice and water. The change of temperature will cause the air pressure inside the bottle to reduce and the bottle will collapse because of the air pressure outside.

Tell the students that even though we can't see it, air does have weight and it does have force. As objects move through air, they meet air friction, just like solid objects moving against other solid objects. This air friction is also called air resistance.

Slowing down

Just as two solid surfaces rubbing against each other produce friction, so too do objects moving through air. The particles of air rub against the object causing friction or resistance and slow it down. An object with a large surface area moving through air will meet more air resistance than one with a smaller surface area.

Demonstrate this principle by asking the students to run across the playground. *That was easy, wasn't it?* Now increase their surface area by asking them to run back holding a large piece of card in front of them. They should find it more difficult and slower going because they are meeting increased resistance from the air pushing back against a larger surface area.

Streamlined shapes

Just as there is resistance in air, there is resistance in water too. As you've demonstrated with the card, large flat shapes have difficulty moving through air and the same is true in water. There are many examples of how marine animals overcome this because of their narrow, pointed bodies, ideally suited to moving quickly through water. They offer very little surface area at the front so cut through the water easily.

When humans have wanted to move faster, we have copied these streamlined shapes to reduce our friction in water and air.

In contrast, because there is no air in space and no particles to create friction, space stations and satellites can be any shape at all; they have no need for streamlining.

Things to do

Fly a kite

A kite does not have to be complicated; it can be as simple as an opened-up plastic carrier bag attached to a length of string.

Record

Hang decorative kites from the ceiling and as the students discover more facts about air resistance, they can add them as fact files to their 'tails'.

Support

Help the students to get the kites airborne and to realize that the force they feel pulling on the kite is just moving air. This should help them appreciate that objects moving through air can meet considerable force.

Extend

Students might like to investigate different styles of kite or construct kites of different sizes and materials.

Windy weather

If possible, link this activity with investigations in geography.

Support

Students may be able to relate wind strength to something like washing hanging on a line. On a calm day, the washing hangs down; on a windier day, it will blow up following the direction of the wind. The Beaufort scale is a measurement of this. Give students a strip of paper and ask them to blow on it. The paper moves higher the more they blow. This is the principle behind the wind gauge.

Extend

The Beaufort scale is often represented pictorially for students (pictures of smoke rising, etc.). However, some students may want to be more accurate and quantifiable. Help them construct a gauge using a shoe box with open ends and a piece of paper suspended from a pencil or rod inside it. Draw a scale on the side of the box. *Does it matter what sort of paper you use? Why?*

Exploring

Students could do some research to explore the relationships between surface area and air resistance in parachutes.

Did you know?

Kites and parachutes are both centuries-old inventions that students could research.

I wonder...

Water resistance is caused by an object having to move water out of the way in order to travel through it. The smaller the point of contact at the front of the object, the less water it will need to move and the less water resistance it will encounter. Torpedo-shaped submarines will use less energy and be more efficient than cubes or spheres.

Other ideas

WS 72

Flying high

Ask students to investigate what makes a good paper plane. Students love throwing paper planes around so to have a legitimate scientific reason for doing so cannot fail to generate enthusiasm! *Think about how the design or position of the wings, or the distribution of the weight, will affect how well your plane can fly.* The students can use WS 72 for a design. Organize a friendly competition to see whose plane can stay in the air the longest.

Presentation

Ask the students to imagine that they are a newspaper reporter for the *Renaissance Times*. It's 1495 and they've set up an interview with a local inventor, Leonardo da Vinci. He claims to have invented a parachute device that will bring a man safely to Earth from huge heights without injury. Encourage the students to use word-processing software to write a report on this new invention, explaining the science behind the idea.

At home

Ask the students to look in their local paper for weather reports that include the speeds of the wind. *Can you find any reports about extreme wind conditions such as hurricanes or tornadoes?*

Plenary

Prepare two different-sized parachutes (made from bin bags and thread), each with an equal load attached, e.g. a washer or piece of plasticine. Remember to cut a small hole in the centre of the canopy to keep the descent even. Ask the students to predict which parachute will fall the fastest. Can they explain why, in terms of friction and air resistance?

115

Unit 6: Friction – Testing spinners

The objectives for this lesson are that students should be able to:

- Observe natural spinners and discover how they 'fly'

- Make their own spinners for testing

- Find out which is the best spinner

- Compare their method and results to those in the *Student Book*.

SB pp.90–91

Starter

- Display a photograph of a flying seed or a real one if available. *Can you see why these seeds can be called 'helicopters'?* Can the students think of any more examples of seeds that travel in the wind?

The challenge

Read the challenge and conversations on page 90 of the *Student Book* and discuss how the seed could have travelled. Explain that you are going to make models of a seed like this and see which one works best.

What to do

Decide what the class means by 'best'. This in itself can generate a very interesting debate. 'Staying in the air longest' is a useful starting point, although your class may have equally reasonable ideas about what 'best' could mean. Just be sure that the ideas they choose can be measured or quantified in some way.

Cut out a basic spinner and demonstrate how it works. It is critically important to fold a spinner into a 'Y' shape. If the wings are folded too far – into a 'T' shape – the spinner will not be stable.

Brainstorm all of the possible ways that the students could change the spinner. Write all the ideas on the board. You may be surprised by just how many the students come up with. To reinforce the scientific method, choose the same variable to change initially, e.g. the type of paper the spinner is made from. After that, each group or pair could test a different modification.

What you need

WS 73

- spinner instructions on WS 73

- scissors

- selection of papers

- paper clips

- a seconds timer

- a measuring stick or tape

Even if students reach up as high as they can to drop their spinners, they won't achieve a drop of more than about 2 metres at the most. Although the spinners will work, they may find such a swift descent difficult to time accurately. If you can raise the students up even slightly, e.g. by safely standing on a PE bench, results will improve.

What to check

Support

If all the students make modifications to the basic spinner design, all other variables must remain the same. The students need to be certain about just what they are testing. For example, if you change the length of the wings, then you must keep the type of paper the same throughout. If, however, you change the type of paper the spinner is made from, you must keep the shape the same. There are endless possibilities here and most will give you interesting and valid results.

Extend

Extension work here lends itself to outcome rather than task. There are so many possibilities that more able students may be able to work through several.

What did you find?

Record

The students should write about their spinners and then use this data to create bar charts or line graphs from their information.

Present

Encourage the students to make a PowerPoint presentation to 'tell the story' of the chart or graph. *Which was the most successful spinner? Which the least?* If students have recorded with a camera or video, they could import clips into their presentations.

Can you do better?

Ask students to show how good their evidence was. How could they tackle the investigation differently if they were starting again? Show the students the results in the *Student Book*. Read it together. *Do you think the results are accurate? Should the investigation have been repeated as there were problems with the tissue paper and thin card spinners? Did we have any of these problems? What did we do about them?*

Now predict

Look for an understanding that it is air friction which affects the descent of the spinner. Gravity is the force that pulls the spinner to Earth but air resistance is the force that slows it down. As the weight of the spinner increases, the spinner will fall more quickly. If the students drop their spinners from a greater height, the spinners are more susceptible to being blown by draughts during a long descent.

The design of flying seeds enables them to stay in the air for a long time and thus be carried a distance away from the parent plant.

Other ideas

Windy fish

Variations on the spinner idea are likely to catch the students' imaginations, including flying fish and windmills. Encourage the students to make and decorate these paper toys that work using the same principles as the spinners.

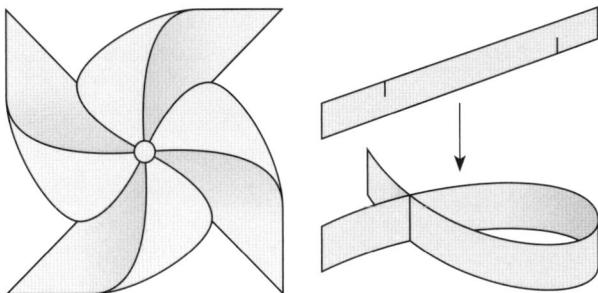

ICT ideas

Students should use spreadsheets to record and compare their results. Results could then be transferred to a graphic program to construct either line graphs or bar charts. If you have a light gate, you could use this to record the spinners' time in the air more accurately.

At home

Ask the students to hunt for airborne seeds. Invite them to bring them to school to make a class collection of different wind-blown seeds. Link this to their understanding of seed dispersal.

Plenary

Invite pairs or groups of students to share their findings with the class and combine the best results of all the investigations to construct a 'super spinner'. *How does your spinner compare to the seed? What is so good about the design of the seed?* There is a good balance of wing and weight that ensures that it flies well and far.

Unit 6: Friction – Exploring friction

The objectives for this lesson are that students should be able to:

- Look at streamlined shapes and learn how they reduce friction

- Find out which shapes are the most streamlined

- Make predictions on the results

- Plan and carry out a fair test.

SB pp.92–93

Starter

- Display several photographs of marine animals, e.g. dolphins, sharks, fish. *What makes these animals so fast through the water?* Elicit ideas to do with their streamlined shapes, which reduce resistance in water.

- Tell the students that they are going to explore which shapes are the most streamlined.

The challenge

Read the conversation on page 92 of the *Student Book* and discuss the boys' ideas. Do the students agree with the boys' ideas? If not, why not?

What to do

Decide how to organize your test. Is everyone going to produce the same shapes to test? Encourage students to predict the outcome of the experiment before they start. *Which shapes do you think would be the most and least streamlined? Why?*

Encourage the more able students to be precise in their experimental method and to repeat each test a number of times so that they can work out an average result.

What you need

- a long tube or a transparent pop bottle with the top cut off

- pieces of plasticine of the same mass, moulded into various shapes, e.g. sphere, cube, torpedo, flat square, dome, etc.

- thin school cold-water paste or another clear, safe viscous fluid – do not use wallpaper paste that contains fungicide

- thread

- a stopwatch or timer

- a digital camera (optional)

- weighing scales

The object of the experiment is to see which shapes move through a liquid more quickly and have least water resistance. Although you could do this experiment using water, plasticine will sink very quickly and the results may be almost too fast for students to time accurately. A better alternative is to use a watery mixture of cold-water paste or another clear, viscous fluid. The shapes will sink slower and you'll have more differentiation between the times. However, getting the thickness right takes a bit of trial and error. Remember that paste thickens up after a while so take this into account if you prepare it in advance. Too thick and all of your shapes will sit on the surface!

To save on the inevitable mess, bury a long, thin piece of thread inside each shape. This will allow you to pull the shape out of the paste without putting your hands in it.

What to check

Encourage students to drop each shape from the same position and to measure the times precisely. Students should time from the same point each time, probably just above the surface of the liquid, which could be marked on the side of the container.

Support

Make sure that the students are timing from the same point each time, using the same units. Use a video camera to record the descents.

Extend

Most students should recognize that the smaller the surface area of the leading edge of the shape, the quicker it travels through the liquid and the less resistance it produces.

Let students experiment using other liquids of different viscosities, e.g. cooking oil, bubble bath or syrup. Use a long narrow tube such as a large measuring cylinder to reduce the amount of liquid needed, otherwise the activity can become costly.

What did you find?
WS 74

Record

The students could record their data in the table provided on WS 74, then transfer this data to create bar charts from their information. As a fallback, they could use the data in the *Student Book*. The shape of plasticine should be on the x-axis and the time of descent on the y-axis.

Present

Ask the students to look at their charts and to tell the story of the graph. *The flatter-fronted shapes moved more slowly than the long, thin shapes.* Encourage them to write what they did and what they saw, including drawing the equipment used, table of results and chart.

Can you do better?

Ask students how good their evidence was. How could they tackle the investigation differently if they were starting again?

Look at the results in the *Student Book. Have the right conclusions been drawn from the results? Were there any surprises? Was there anything that could have been done better?*

Now predict

Look for an understanding that streamlined shapes move more quickly through fluids than shapes that are flatter or wider. The more streamlined a shape, the less resistance it produces. Students should also understand that the liquid used will make a difference to the time taken, but should not necessarily affect the order of the results.

Other ideas

Torpedo races

Have a class torpedo race from the top to the bottom of paste-filled tubes. The first to the bottom wins!

ICT ideas

Students could record their results on a spreadsheet and use this to compile an average of several readings. Information could be entered into the graphing program and used to draw different types of chart. Remind students that both axes should have labels and that their graphs must have titles.

At home
WS 75

Ask the students to use secondary sources to find out how various sports overcome water resistance. Suggest that they look at sailing, surfing, diving, waterskiing or swimming. Back in school, discuss the types of equipment sportspeople use and their design. *How do special sports clothes help reduce resistance?*

Ask students to complete WS 75.

Plenary

The ideal way to round off the topic would be to go swimming and test out some of the concepts safely in deeper water. If this is not possible, use secondary sources to discover the fastest swimming speeds of some marine animals. Compile a chart showing speeds of dolphins, sharks, fish, etc. and discuss what makes them so speedy in water. Mackerel can swim at 30 km per hour, barracuda at 40 km per hour, flying fish at 60 km per hour, sharks at 70 km per hour, swordfish at 90 km per hour and blue fin tuna at a staggering 100 km per hour!

119

Unit 6: Friction – Unit 6 Review

The objectives for this lesson are that students should be able to:

- Check what they have learned about friction in this Unit

- Find out how they are working within the Grade 3 level.

SB p.94 **Expectations**

Students working towards Grade 3 level will:

- Identify friction as a force

- Describe some ways in which friction between solid surfaces can be increased

- Identify some trends or patterns in observations and measurements

- Measure forces simply.

In addition, students working within Grade 3 level will:

- Describe some of the factors that increase air and water resistance

- Describe how to measure forces

- Recognize that forces can start or stop objects moving

- Describe how forces change the shape of objects

- Recognize what friction does to objects

- Describe how to investigate friction, explaining what their results show

- Relate what they found out to their everyday experience

- Present their results in a variety of ways.

Further to this, students working beyond Grade 3 level will also:

- Describe situations in which frictional forces are helpful as well as those in which frictional forces resist motion

- Describe in general how to increase or overcome frictional forces in everyday situations.

Check-up

Farida will have to wear special clothes to make her body shape as streamlined as possible. Her clothes will need to be tight-fitting, so that nothing will flap in the wind and cause resistance. Her bike helmet should present a streamlined shape so that the air is swept back over her head.

Assessment

WS 76

Use the Unit 6 assessment on WS 76 to check the students' understanding of the content of the Unit. The answers are given opposite.

Name: _____ Date: _____

WS 76 **Unit 6 assessment**

1 Sanjay was sledging down a snowy slope when he ran into a patch of grass where the snow had melted. What would happen to the speed of the sledge and why?

2 Here are some results of an experiment to see which shoes had the most grip.

a) Which shoes had the most grip?

b) Which shoe had the most slippery sole?

3 Look at these vehicles.

a) Which would have the most air resistance? Why?

b) Which would have the least? Why?

4 Give one example of where friction is useful to us.

5 Give one example of where friction is unhelpful.

Answers

1   The sledge would slow down because a grass surface has greater friction than an icy surface.

2   **a**   The wellington boot had most grip.

    b   The ballet shoe had the most slippery sole.

3   **a**   The lorry, because it is not streamlined.

    b   The car, because it is streamlined.

4   Accept any reasonable example, e.g. walking, grips on handlebars, playing a game of air hockey, etc.

5   Accept any reasonable example, e.g. friction between moving parts in an engine.

The answer!

Refer back to the Unit question about Haniya's grandad. Discuss how the students now know that smooth surfaces, particularly when they are lubricated with something like oil or water, have low frictional forces and can be very slippery. To increase the friction on solid surfaces, we need to keep the surfaces dry and use high-friction materials such as carpet or rubber to stop us slipping.

And finally...

Make a 'sports scene' wall display. Include field sports, gymnastics, athletics, motor sports, winter sports and water sports. Indicate the aspects of each sport that either enhance or reduce friction, e.g. rubber hand-grips on racquets, grips on goalkeepers' gloves, chalk on gymnasts' hands, etc. Label each aspect with a question, e.g. Why do swimmers wear caps? Why do running shoes have spikes? Why does a snooker player chalk his cue? Display a selection of sports and PE equipment to support the questions.